The Book of Amos

The Book of Amos

Jason R. Jackson

Printed in the United States of America
Cover design by Strange Last Name
Page design by PerfecType, Nashville, Tennessee

Jackson, Jason R.
  The Book of Amos / Jason R. Jackson. – Frankin, Tennessee : Seedbed Publishing, ©2018.

     pages ; cm. + 1 videodisc – (OneBook. Daily-weekly)

  An eight-week Bible study.
  ISBN 9781628245660 (paperback)
  ISBN 9781628245707 (DVD)
  ISBN 9781628245677 (Mobi)
  ISBN 9781628245684 (ePub)
  ISBN 9781628245691 (uPDF)

  1. Bible. Amos -- Textbooks. 2. Bible. Amos -- Study and teaching. 3. Bible. Amos -- Commentaries.   I. Title. II. Series.

BS1585.55.J33 2018   224/.806   2018951692

SEEDBED PUBLISHING
Franklin, Tennessee
seedbed.com

For Sarah—my wife and spiritual friend—
and our daughters: Cora, Avi, and Lilah,
stay salty and shine brightly!

CONTENTS

WELCOME TO ONEBOOK DAILY-WEEKLY

John Wesley, in a letter to one of his leaders, penned the following:

> O begin! Fix some part of every day for private exercises. You may acquire the taste which you have not: what is tedious at first, will afterwards be pleasant. Whether you like it or not, read and pray daily. It is for your life; there is no other way; else you will be a trifler all your days. . . . Do justice to your own soul; give it time and means to grow. Do not starve yourself any longer. Take up your cross and be a Christian altogether.

Rarely are our lives most shaped by our biggest ambitions and highest aspirations. Rather, our lives are most shaped, for better or for worse, by those small things we do every single day.

At Seedbed, our biggest ambition and highest aspiration is to resource the followers of Jesus to become lovers and doers of the Word of God every single day, to become people of One Book.

To that end, we have created the OneBook Daily-Weekly. First, it's important to understand what this is not: warm, fuzzy, sentimental devotions. If you engage the Daily-Weekly for any length of time, you will learn the Word of God. You will grow profoundly in your love for God, and you will become a passionate lover of people.

How Does the Daily-Weekly Work?

Daily. As the name implies, every day invites a short but substantive engagement with the Bible. Five days a week you will read a passage of Scripture followed by a short segment of teaching and closing with a question for reflection and self-examination. On the sixth day, you will review and reflect on the previous five days.

Weekly. Each week, on the seventh day, find a way to gather with at least one other person doing the study. Pursue the weekly guidance for gathering. Share learning, insight, encouragement, and most importantly, how the Holy Spirit is working in your lives.

That's it. Depending on the length of the study, when the eight or twelve weeks are done, we will be ready with the next study. On an ongoing basis we will release new editions of the Daily-Weekly. Over time, those who pursue this course of learning will develop a rich library of Bible learning resources for the long haul.

OneBook Daily-Weekly will develop eight- and twelve-week studies that cover the entire Old and New Testaments. Seedbed will publish new studies regularly so that an ongoing supply of group lessons will be available. All titles will remain accessible, which means they can be used in any order that fits your needs or the needs of your group.

If you are looking for a substantive study to learn Scripture through a steadfast method, look no further.

Amos 1–3 and 7

The World of Amos

ONE

Costly Prosperity

Amos 1:1 NRSV *The words of Amos, who was among the shepherds of Tekoa, which he saw concerning Israel in the days of King Uzziah of Judah and in the days of King Jeroboam son of Joash of Israel, two years before the earthquake.*

2 Kings 14:23–29 NRSV *In the fifteenth year of King Amaziah son of Joash of Judah, King Jeroboam son of Joash of Israel began to reign in Samaria; he reigned forty-one years. 24He did what was evil in the sight of the LORD; he did not depart from all the sins of Jeroboam son of Nebat, which he caused Israel to sin. 25He restored the border of Israel from Lebo-hamath as far as the Sea of the Arabah, according to the word of the LORD, the God of Israel, which he spoke by his servant Jonah son of Amittai, the prophet, who was from Gath-hepher. 26For the LORD saw that the distress of Israel was very bitter; there was no one left, bond or free, and no one to help Israel. 27But the LORD had not said that he would blot out the name of Israel from under heaven, so he saved them by the hand of Jeroboam son of Joash.*

28Now the rest of the acts of Jeroboam, and all that he did, and his might, how he fought, and how he recovered for Israel Damascus and Hamath, which had belonged to Judah, are they not written in the Book of the Annals of the Kings of Israel? 29Jeroboam slept with his ancestors, the kings of Israel; his son Zechariah succeeded him.

Key Observation. For God's people, prosperity cannot come at the expense of faithfulness to God or justice for others.

Understanding the Word. Welcome to Amos! I'm excited and honestly impressed you're studying an Old Testament prophet. These folks can be intimidating, a bit disturbing, and difficult to understand. For starters, it's hard to track the prophets and the kings that they name. The biblical writers certainly didn't make it easy for us. They wrote about Israel's kings in some books and the prophets' words to those kings in different books. For instance, 2 Kings summarizes the reign of the kings that Amos addresses. In this study, we'll read Amos in conversation with other biblical sources to get the whole picture.

To understand a prophet's words, we also have to understand his world. At the time of Amos, God's people were divided into two kingdoms. This split happened two generations after King David. His son Solomon amassed substantial wealth, obtained international fame, and built magnificent buildings, including a temple in Jerusalem. But his achievements came at a price. To solidify his alliances, he married foreign women, who led him to worship other gods. To build his structures, he oppressed those living in the north. His prosperity had spiritual and social ramifications. Political and economic success often does.

After Solomon died, his son Rehoboam became king. The northern tribes begged him to lighten their load, but he refused. So, they split and made Jeroboam, the son of Nebat, their king. The Northern Kingdom kept the name Israel. The Southern Kingdom took the name of its biggest tribe—Judah.

Jeroboam immediately established a new capital in Shechem and alternative worship centers in Dan and Bethel. (Amos has a lot to say about Bethel.) He crafted a golden calf for each sanctuary and directed Israel to offer sacrifices to them. This violated the second commandment not to make idols (Exodus 20:4–6). Jeroboam led Israel to do this for twenty-two years, and the rest of Israel's kings did the same.

About 125 years later, another Jeroboam became Israel's king. Jeroboam, the son of Joash, ruled for forty-one years while Amaziah and Uzziah reigned in Judah. During their tenures, both kingdoms enjoyed a time of peace and prosperity. They got along with each other, and neither worried about the region's traditional superpowers. Babylon and Egypt's power had declined. Assyria had started to rebound, but this temporarily benefited Israel.

At the end of the previous century, the Assyrians conquered Damascus, the capital of the Arameans in Syria. This weakened Israel's northern foe and allowed them to regain territory along important trade routes. An economic boom followed. Trade soared. Cities flourished. Everything looked glorious, but Israel's growth benefited some and cost others.

A sizable gap emerged between the rich and the poor as the upper class used their power and resources for personal gain. They oppressed the poor. They perverted justice. They violated God's law and filled their lives with leisure. They prospered, but others paid.

Therefore, God raised up a generation of prophets to address the problem. Amos was the first. He spoke within a particular situation, but his words go beyond his time. God's people have preserved and passed them on for thousands of years. Our task is to understand his words in their historical context and then apply them to ours. As we go along, we'll find Amos's world is not that different from ours.

1. What would make you feel prosperous or successful?

2. Do you feel comfortable asking God for things that would make you prosperous or successful? Why or why not?

T W O

An Uninvited Voice

Amos 1:1 NRSV *The words of Amos, who was among the shepherds of Tekoa, which he saw concerning Israel in the days of King Uzziah of Judah and in the days of King Jeroboam son of Joash of Israel, two years before the earthquake.*

Amos 7:12–15 NRSV *And Amaziah said to Amos, "O seer, go, flee away to the land of Judah, earn your bread there, and prophesy there; 13but never again prophesy at Bethel, for it is the king's sanctuary, and it is a temple of the kingdom."*

14Then Amos answered Amaziah, "I am no prophet, nor a prophet's son; but I am a herdsman, and a dresser of sycamore trees, 15and the LORD took me from following the flock, and the LORD said to me, 'Go, prophesy to my people Israel.'"

Key Observation. God calls his people to speak against injustice even when it's not wanted or welcomed.

Understanding the Word. These verses contain everything we know about Amos himself. It's not much, but it helps us connect with the man behind the message. He ministered two years before an earthquake in mid-700s BC. Zechariah mentions the same earthquake (14:5), but we're not sure when it happened. Nevertheless, the reference does narrow Amos's unusually short career to a particular, albeit unknown, year during the reigns of Uzziah (783–742 BC) and Jeroboam II (786–746 BC).

Before God called him, Amos was a shepherd, a herdsman, and a tree farmer. In the original language (Hebrew), the word translated "shepherd" is used only one other time, where it describes King Mesha of Moab—a nation east of Judah (2 Kings 3:4). Mesha routinely gave Israel's king a massive number of lambs and a mammoth amount of wool as political tribute. This suggests that Amos oversaw a large-scale herding and breeding operation. Combined with his sycamore business, Amos was probably well off. But unlike Israel's financial elite, Amos earned his wealth ethically.

Amos prophesied in Israel, but he wasn't an Israelite. He was from Judah. Tekoa was a small town a few miles south of Jerusalem. God sent him across the border to Bethel, which housed one of Jeroboam I's golden calves. There Amos butted heads with a priest named Amaziah. Amos challenged Amaziah's worldview, jeopardized his livelihood, and threatened his king. Consequently, Amaziah told Amos to skedaddle. Amos wasn't wanted or welcomed in Israel. Prophets never were.

During this conversation, Amos apparently denied being a prophet. But being the son of a prophet didn't mean you came from a long line of prophets. Instead, it meant that you had completed a prophetic training program and now earned a living speaking for God. (Imagine that for a moment.)

Ancient kings kept professional prophets on their payrolls. To keep their jobs, paid prophets typically said what their kings wanted to hear rather than what the Lord wanted to say. In this light, Amos's statement was more like a declaration of his independence than a denial of his calling. He essentially told Amaziah, "I'm not your run-of-the-mill royal prophet. I've been called by God, not hired by a king."

This is a huge distinction! True prophets don't tickle the ears of those who pay their bills. They speak God's words regardless of the danger or the cost. True prophets don't cave to power; they oppose it with the power of God. They give voice to the voiceless and call oppressors to repent. Unfortunately, people in power usually resist change, especially when it threatens their way of life. Instead, they squelch the messenger. This is why true prophets are rarely invited, often persecuted, and sometimes killed in action. Persecution isn't the goal, but it is a vocational hazard.

If this has ever happened to you, you're in good company. Jesus experienced this kind of treatment and told us to expect the same. He said, "Blessed are you when people revile you and persecute you and utter all kinds of evil against you falsely on my account. Rejoice and be glad, for your reward is great in heaven, for in the same way they persecuted the prophets who were before you" (Matt. 5:11–12 NRSV).

1. What did you previously think a prophet was or a prophet did?

2. Who is someone that you would consider to be a modern-day prophet? How have they challenged you or others?

THREE

The Lord's Roar

Amos 1:2–3a NRSV *And he said: The* Lord *roars from Zion, and utters his voice from Jerusalem; the pastures of the shepherds wither, and the top of Carmel dries up.* ³*Thus says the* Lord*: . . .*

Amos 3:3–8 NRSV *Do two walk together unless they have made an appointment?* ⁴*Does a lion roar in the forest, when it has no prey? Does a young lion cry out from its den, if it has caught nothing?* ⁵*Does a bird fall into a snare on the earth, when there is no trap for it? Does a snare spring up from the ground, when it has taken nothing?* ⁶*Is a trumpet blown in a city, and the people are not afraid? Does disaster befall a city, unless the* Lord *has done it?* ⁷*Surely the Lord* God *does nothing, without revealing his secret to his servants the prophets.* ⁸*The lion has roared; who will not fear? The Lord* God *has spoken; who can but prophesy?*

Key Observation. God's wrath is utterly good; it confronts evil and overturns injustice.

Understanding the Word. Verse 2 is Amos's theme verse. It grabs our attention and sets the stage for everything that follows. Here Amos graphically depicts the Lord as a roaring lion. As a lion's roar evokes despair in its prey (Amos 3:4–8), we can anticipate that God's words will do the same in Israel. Throughout Amos, God will confront rather than comfort his people. In the same way, as we read this book together, God will challenge us more often than he'll console us. (Aren't you glad you chose this study?)

Amos 1:2–3 introduces us to two important features of Israelite prophecy. The first is a structure commonly used in biblical Hebrew poetry called *parallelism*. Most of Israel's prophetic literature is poetic in nature, so we'll see this a lot in Amos. English poetry is generally characterized by rhyming. We repeat sounds, as in "Jack and *Jill* went up the *hill.*" Hebrew poetry rarely rhymes. Instead, it restates, contrasts, or expands ideas or images from one line to the next. For example, in verse 2, "roar" is paralleled by "utters his voice" and "from Zion" by "from Jerusalem." The second line restates the first.

The second feature—"Thus says the LORD"—is known as the *messenger formula*. These words signal that Amos is God's messenger. The words he speaks are not his own; they're the Lord's. Though this book bears the name of Amos, it contains the word of God. These are God's words to God's people—to Israel, to you, and to me.

In Amos, the Lord's voice rises from Jerusalem (a.k.a. Zion). He doesn't speak to the Northern Kingdom from their sanctuaries in Dan and Bethel. Instead, he speaks to them from the capital city of the Southern Kingdom, where Solomon built his temple. Like Amos himself, God's words come to Israel from Judah. All of this suggests that God's indictments against Israel will focus on her worship centers.

When the Lord roars, fire follows. The grass withers, and the mountains dry up. The Bible often represents God's wrath with fire. Amos will liken them often. In tomorrow's reading, he'll portray God's anger burning against several foreign nations (1:3–2:3). Then on Day Five, Amos will envision God setting parts of Judah ablaze. But in Amos 1:2, as well as 5:6 and 7:4, his wrath consumes the entire Northern Kingdom. As we read, we'll encounter God's absolute and final judgment of Israel.

If we're being honest, the subject of God's wrath unsettles us. It seems incompatible with his love and mercy. We typically think that God is either one or the other. But Amos will remind us that God is both/and. He's good *and* great, gracious *and* holy, merciful *and* just. These traits are not mutually exclusive with God, even though they often are with us.

When we judge, our judgments can be biased, self-serving, and vindictive. They can make things worse, rather than set things right. But when God judges, he's fair, just, and good. His judgments are consistent with his character and unbiased. He condemns evil and enacts justice. He does what we cannot. Even though his wrath disturbs us, it is ultimately good for us.

1. What typically comes to mind when you think about God's wrath or judgment? Who does God judge? Why?

2. How does this passage and reflection influence your beliefs about God's judgment?

FOUR

All Nations under God

Amos 1:3–8 NRSV *Thus says the LORD: For three transgressions of Damascus, and for four, I will not revoke the punishment; because they have threshed Gilead with threshing sledges of iron. ⁴So I will send a fire on the house of Hazael, and it shall devour the strongholds of Ben-hadad. ⁵I will break the gate bars of Damascus, and cut off the inhabitants from the Valley of Aven, and the one who holds the scepter from Beth-eden; and the people of Aram shall go into exile to Kir, says the LORD.*

⁶Thus says the LORD: For three transgressions of Gaza, and for four, I will not revoke the punishment; because they carried into exile entire communities, to hand them over to Edom. ⁷So I will send a fire on the wall of Gaza, fire that shall devour its strongholds. ⁸I will cut off the inhabitants from Ashdod, and the one who holds the scepter from Ashkelon; I will turn my hand against Ekron, and the remnant of the Philistines shall perish, says the Lord GOD.

Key Observation. The Lord's power and protection encompass *all* nations.

Understanding the Word. After Amos's opening image, the Lord pronounces judgment on seven of Israel's neighbors. He begins with the Arameans (Damascus) in the northeast (1:3–5). Then he jumps down to the Philistines (Gaza) in the southwest (1:6–8). Next, he moves up the Mediterranean coast to the Phoenicians (Tyre) in the northwest (1:9–10). His focus then shifts across to Edom (1:11–12), Ammon (1:13–15), and Moab (2:1–3) in the south and east. Eventually, he narrows his gaze on Judah (2:4–5). If you're an Israelite, you probably feel relieved after Amos's roaring lion bit. But the longer he talks, you realize the Lord's judgment is spiraling inward. At some point, you realize you're the bull's-eye.

The seven oracles against the nations all follow a similar pattern. They begin with the messenger formula—"Thus says the LORD"—followed by a number sentence—"for three transgressions of [nation or representative city] and for four, I will not revoke punishment." Amos then names one transgression and delivers the Lord's discipline. He'll burn down their strongholds and go from there. Most of the pronouncements conclude with a second "Thus says the LORD" for emphasis.

Amos denounces the nations for what they've done to other people. They probably committed these acts during war. Nevertheless, the Lord chastises them for what we would call "war crimes": mistreating the vulnerable (e.g., pregnant women) (1:13) and betraying their allies (1:9).

The Arameans and Ammonites brutalized the people of Gilead (1:3, 13). The Philistines and Phoenicians profited from selling captives to Edom (1:6, 9). The Edomites perpetually set themselves against their brother Judah (1:11; Genesis 36:1). The Moabites grossly mistreated the remains of Edom's king (Amos 2:1). Collectively, they used their military strength to commit human atrocities, and they broke their international commitments for national gain.

Therefore, the Lord will destroy their defenses and make them vulnerable to attack. He'll also send the Arameans back to Kir (1:5 and 9:7). He'll eliminate the Philistines (1:8). He'll drive out Amon's leaders (1:15) and destroy the Moab's officials (2:3). In light of each nation's named trespasses, the Lord's judgments are just. His punishments fit their crimes.

Originally, the most startling aspect of these speeches would have been their international dimension. In the ancient world, people believed in many gods. They associated these gods with specific natural forces or geographic regions. The gods couldn't operate outside of their designated spheres. But according to Amos, Israel's God is sovereign over every nation. The Lord's power and care extend beyond Israel and Judah's borders. He can cause any nation's demise and use any country to do his bidding. Ultimately, he'll judge every state according to universal standards like keeping promises and protecting the weak.

Today, our world is fraught with international tension and conflict. Border disputes, civil wars, economic sanctions, religious extremism, global espionage, election tampering, missile tests, and forced migrations fill our news cycles. Confusion and fear seem to reign in our age. But Amos reminds us it is the Lord who rules over all. He invites us to trust that God can and will enact justice and establish peace on earth.

1. How is God's sovereignty over all nations good news to you today? How does it challenge you?

2. Are there particular nations who you wish were not included in God's care? Would you be willing to pray for them right now?

FIVE

The Good King

Amos 2:4–5 NRSV *Thus says the Lord: For three transgressions of Judah, and for four, I will not revoke the punishment; because they have rejected the law of the Lord, and have not kept his statutes, but they have been led astray by the same lies after which their ancestors walked. ⁵So I will send a fire on Judah, and it shall devour the strongholds of Jerusalem.*

2 Kings 15:1–7 NRSV *In the twenty-seventh year of King Jeroboam of Israel King Azariah son of Amaziah of Judah began to reign. ²He was sixteen years old when he began to reign, and he reigned fifty-two years in Jerusalem. His mother's name was Jecoliah of Jerusalem. ³He did what was right in the sight of the Lord, just as his father Amaziah had done. ⁴Nevertheless the high places were not taken away; the people still sacrificed and made offerings on the high places. ⁵The Lord struck the king, so that he was leprous to the day of his death, and lived in a* *separate house. Jotham the king's son was in charge of the palace, governing the people of the land. ⁶Now the rest of the acts of Azariah, and all that he did, are they not written in the Book of the Annals of the Kings of Judah? ⁷Azariah slept with his ancestors; they buried him with his ancestors in the city of David; his son Jotham succeeded him.*

Key Observation. Good leaders do what is right *and* teach others to do the same.

Understanding the Word. We generally assume Israel's prophets predicted events in the far-off future. They actually did more forth-telling than fore-telling. The prophets revealed how God felt about the *present*. They called God's people to change and warned them what would happen if they refused. When they did predict the future, it was usually a near future.

Today's passage is the last in the series of oracles against other nations. Yesterday, we saw how with each speech God's judgment drew closer to Israel. But just before he settles in, the Lord somewhat surprisingly confronts Judah and foreshadows her fate.

We know from Day One of this week that all of the Northern Kingdom's kings followed Jeroboam I's example and led Israel to worship idols. The Southern Kingdom's kings were a bit of a mixed bag. Some "did what was right in the eyes of the LORD" (2 Kings 15:3); others did not. Amos prophesied during the reign of King Uzziah (a.k.a. Azariah). Uzziah was a good king, but he notably failed to remove the "high places" (15:4).

High places were local worship centers where people regularly honored idols. The Lord hated them. He told his people to destroy them as soon as they entered the land he promised to their ancestor Abraham (Numbers 33:52). But they didn't (1 Kings 3:2–4). Solomon even constructed new ones to worship other gods (1 Kings 11:7).

After the kingdoms split, Solomon's son Rehoboam erected even more of them *in Judah* (1 Kings 14:23). This is exactly what Jeroboam I did *in Israel*. Bethel was a high place (1 Kings 12:32)! Only two of Judah's kings tore down the high places—Hezekiah (2 Kings 18:4) and Josiah (2 Kings 23:8). These kings did what was right *and* led others to do the same. They're the kind of kings God wants.

Though God sends Amos north to Israel, he's not letting Judah off the hook. Like Israel, the Lord chose Judah to represent him. Their election came with expectations. He judges them for failing to fulfill their obligations to him. They followed their forefathers' folly rather than God's laws. As a result, they'll share the other nations' fate. God's anger will ignite their entire land. His fury will scorch Jerusalem's walls.

Less than two hundred years later, what Amos prophesied came to pass. In 587 BC, the Babylonians conquered Judah's capital. They destroyed its walls and its temple. They deported its king and most of its citizens. Years later, Judah returned and rebuilt the temple, but things were never quite the same. Therefore, God's people began to hope that he would send them a new king to restore their fortunes.

Eventually, God did! His Son Jesus descended from King David (Matthew 1:1). He was the rightful heir to Judah's throne. He proclaimed the return of God's kingdom and called people to renew their allegiance to God (Matthew 4:17). He did what was right *and* taught others to do the same. He obeyed all the way to death on the cross. Therefore, God raised him from the dead, elevated him above all, and called the nations to worship him as the King over all kings (Philippians 2:6–11).

1. Who are the people in your life who did what was right and taught you to do the same?

2. Who are the people that you're leading? Can they say that you both lead by example and teach them to do the same?

WEEK ONE

GATHERING DISCUSSION OUTLINE

A. Open session in prayer.

B. View this week's video.

C. What general impressions and thoughts do you have after watching the video and reading the daily writings on these Scriptures? What, specifically, did this week's passages teach you about faith, life, and prayer?

D. Discuss selected questions from the daily readings. Always invite class members to share key insights or to raise questions that they found to be the most meaningful.

1. **KEY OBSERVATION**: For God's people, prosperity cannot come at the expense of faithfulness to God or justice for others.

   DISCUSSION QUESTION: Do you feel comfortable asking God for the things that would make you feel prosperous or successful? Why or why not?

2. **KEY OBSERVATION**: God calls his people to speak against injustice even when it's not wanted or welcomed.

   DISCUSSION QUESTION: Who is someone that you would consider to be a modern-day prophet? How have they challenged you or others?

3. **KEY OBSERVATION:** God's wrath is utterly good; it confronts evil and overturns injustice.

DISCUSSION QUESTION: How does this passage and reflection transform your beliefs about God's judgment?

4. **KEY OBSERVATION:** The Lord's power and protection encompass *all* nations.

   DISCUSSION QUESTION: How is God's sovereignty over all nations good news to you today? How does it challenge you?

5. **KEY OBSERVATION:** Good leaders do what is right *and* teach others to do the same.

   DISCUSSION QUESTION: Who are the people that you're leading? Can they say that you both lead by example and teach them to do the same?

E. Close session with prayer.

Amos 2–3

The State of Israel

ONE

Love and Justice

Amos 2:6–8 *This is what the Lord says: "For three sins of Israel, even for four, I will not relent. They sell the innocent for silver, and the needy for a pair of sandals. ⁷They trample on the heads of the poor as on the dust of the ground and deny justice to the oppressed. Father and son use the same girl and so profane my holy name. ⁸They lie down beside every altar on garments taken in pledge. In the house of their god they drink wine taken as fines."*

Key Observation. We love God rightly when we treat others justly.

Understanding the Word. After pronouncing judgment on seven other nations, the Lord hits his primary target—Israel. This speech opens like the others, but then it deviates from the pattern. God cites Israel for *four* transgressions not just one. They enslave the poor, deny justice to the oppressed, sexually abuse the powerless, and profit from the needy. These are serious violations for any nation. They're particularly egregious in light of Israel's story.

For generations, God's people were slaves in Egypt. Their ancestors had migrated there due to a famine. They initially prospered, but eventually, their population growth threatened Egypt's king. In fear, Pharaoh oppressed Israel, but centuries later, God rescued them. Because he had set them free, the Lord prohibited his people from permanently depriving each other of the freedom *he* gave them.

Whenever a fellow Israelite was in need, the Lord commanded his people to lend to her with zero interest and sell food to her at zero profit (Leviticus 25:35–38). He also told Israel to under harvest their crops and leave what remains for the poor (Deuteronomy 24:19–22). If an Israelite did become seriously indebted, he could sell himself into slavery. However, when he paid the debt, after six years, or in the fifty-year Jubilee, he was set free (Leviticus 25:8–17). Furthermore, God required his people to provide their former slaves with everything they needed for a fresh start (Deuteronomy 15:12–15). How cool is that?

But in Amos, Israel does the opposite. They act like Egyptians instead of like God. They force their fellow Israelites into slavery over minuscule debts. The courts compound the problem by denying the needy a fair trial and depriving them of dignity.

On top of that, Israel allows its men to sexually violate its women. In the ancient world, men had substantially more power than women, but the Lord instituted laws to protect and promote women. For example, he forbade fathers from forcing their daughters-in-laws to have sex with them (Leviticus 18:15). Apparently, this was common at that time. But Israel's dads ignore God's directives and take advantage of their son's wives anyway. This is appalling!

Israel also flaunts its maltreatment of the poor. Whenever an Israelite borrowed money from another, he would leave an item as collateral. If he was poor, he'd leave his cloak—his last possession. Cloaks doubled as blankets, so God ordered lenders to return them each night (Exodus 22:26–27; Deuteronomy 24:10–13). Instead of returning the cloaks, Israel's elite sleep on them.

Additionally, whenever an Israelite harmed someone or their property, he had to pay a fine to make restitution and alleviate suffering (e.g., Exodus 21–22). Instead of distributing these fines to those who were harmed, Israel's powerful purchase wine for themselves and drink it in their sanctuaries. While this may please other gods, despising justice displeases the Lord.

Jesus chastised a group of religious leaders on similar grounds. They gave what the Law required, but they neglected justice *and* the love of God (Luke 11:42). God wants us to adore him *and* to care for others. We can't separate loving God from loving others. In fact, we rightly worship the Lord by doing for others what he's done for us.

1. Who are the poor, oppressed, powerless, and needy in your city?

2. How do people of power and systems of justice treat the poor, oppressed, powerless, and needy in your city? How does the church treat them? How do you treat them?

TWO

Is This Not True?

Amos 2:9–11 *"Yet I destroyed the Amorites before them, though they were tall as the cedars and strong as the oaks. I destroyed their fruit above and their roots below. ¹⁰I brought you up out of Egypt and led you forty years in the wilderness to give you the land of the Amorites.*

¹¹"I also raised up prophets from among your children and Nazirites from among your youths. Is this not true, people of Israel?" declares the LORD.

Key Observation. God expects his grace for us to evoke faithfulness from us.

Understanding the Word. After outlining Israel's atrocities, the Lord employs a popular parenting tactic. Like a father to his ungrateful child, he systematically recounts everything he's done for his people. This litany of God's great acts highlights the gravity of his grievances against them. His loyalty exposes the depth of their infidelity.

The Amorites inhabited Palestine before Israel. They're named alongside the Canaanites, Hittites, Perizzites, Hivites, Jebusites, and all your other favorites (e.g., Judges 3:5). But sometimes the Bible uses "Amorites" to refer to all the "-ites" as a group (e.g., Judges 6:10). In various places, the Amorites and others are described as tall and strong (e.g., Deuteronomy 1:28). Despite their opposing presence, the Lord uprooted them from the land.

Before that, God rescued Israel from Egypt. In the Old Testament, the Lord consistently identifies himself as the God of the exodus. He is the God who saved Israel. He is their God and they are his people. He's personally invested in them, so he takes their offenses personally. We can hear it in his voice as he addresses Israel directly for the first time in these verses.

Then God faithfully led and generously provided for his people as they wandered around the wilderness for forty years. The trip shouldn't have taken that long. But the Israelites went kicking and screaming the whole way. At times, they actually asked to go back to Egypt. They complained about the bitterness of the water (Exodus 15:22–27), the amount and variety of the food (Exodus 16; Numbers 11), and the size of the Amorites (Numbers 13). Yet the Lord sweetened their drink, provided and varied their meals, and cleared their land.

If that wasn't enough, the Lord gave Israel prophets to remind them of his works and Nazirites to inspire them to be faithful to his ways. Nazirites were men and women uniquely dedicated to the Lord (Numbers 6). They grew out their hair, abstained from all things grape, and kept their distance from the dead. They wouldn't even attend family funerals. Their appearance, diet, and avoidance of death demonstrated their commitment to the life-giving God. (See Judges 13:5; 1 Samuel 1:11, 28; Mark 1:6; Acts 18:18; and 21:23 for potential examples.)

Now the Lord, like a loving but exasperated parent, asks his children, "Is this not true?" This is the first of many rhetorical questions in Amos. The answer is obvious, but it's the impact of the answer that really matters. Israel can't deny their history with their lips, even if they deny it with their lives. Their silence reinforces their guilt. God has repeatedly demonstrated his grace to Israel, but they've continually disgraced him.

In the ancient world, there was no such thing as a gift or a grace with no strings attached. Gifts created connections and generated responses. Likewise, God gives his grace to create faithful people (Romans 1:5). He expects it to have an effect on us just as it did on Paul. "His grace to me was not without effect. No, I worked harder than all of them—yet not I, but the grace of God that was with me" (1 Cor. 15:10b). God's grace evoked Paul's faithfulness. It should evoke ours as well.

1. In what ways have you experienced God's grace during this season of your life?

2. How are you faithfully responding to God's grace during this season of your life?

THREE

But You . . .

Amos 2:12–16 *"But you made the Nazirites drink wine and commanded the prophets not to prophesy.*

[13]"Now then, I will crush you as a cart crushes when loaded with grain. [14]The swift will not escape, the strong will not muster their strength, and the warrior will not save his life. [15]The archer will not stand his ground, the fleet-footed soldier will not get away, and the horseman will not save his life. [16]Even the bravest warriors will flee naked on that day," declares the LORD.

Key Observation. Only God can remove the burden of our guilt and lift the weight of his wrath.

Understanding the Word. "I did all of this for you *but you . . .*"—words like this are hard to hear and hard to say. We've all heard our parents, our spouses, our friends, or even our children saying something similar to us or us to them. Despite all the Lord had done for Israel, they made those who devoted themselves to his service break their vows. They forced them to drink wine and forfeit their distinctiveness. They made them as faithless as the rest. They even tried to silence those who speak for God. But prophets can't keep quiet (Amos 3:8), so Amos shouts on God's behalf.

"Now then . . ."—this is a strong interjection in Hebrew. It's Israel's wake-up call. The time has come for them to sit up and pay attention to the Lord speaking through someone they attempted to mute. God follows this exclamation with an emphatic "I." It's as though he were saying, "Now then watch what *I* will do to you on account of all that you've done to me and my people! You've mistreated your fellow Israelites and tarnished my reputation. In the past, you received my grace, but you weren't grateful. Therefore, you will receive my vengeance!"

In the previous oracles against the nations, Amos portrayed God's judgment as a wall-consuming fire. His fury devoured city fortifications and left entire populations vulnerable to enemy attack. But in these verses there is no fire; instead, there's an oppressive and inescapable weight. The immense magnitude of God's wrath will land on Israel and stop them in their faithless tracks.

As Amos continues, he applies this image to various people. His applications illustrate that there's no way Israel can avoid God's judgment. Their fastest will not outrun it. Their strongest will not endure it. Their fiercest will not fend it off. Even their best warriors—their archers, their infantry, and their cavalry—will not evade it. They'll drop their weapons and try to flee, but they won't save themselves or anyone else. Israel's most exceptional citizens and her most prepared soldiers will find themselves hindered and helpless. Everyone, like an overloaded and immobile wagon, will be stymied under the weight of God's certain chastisement.

This weighty imagery isn't unique to Amos. The psalmist employs it in Psalm 32:3–4: "When I kept silent [about my sin], my bones wasted away through my groaning all day long. For day and night your hand was heavy on me; my strength was sapped as in the heat of summer." God's judgment is unwieldy. But Psalm 32 doesn't stop there. The writer goes on to confess his sin. When he does, the Lord forgives him. In Hebrew, the word translated *forgive* literally means to "lift," "carry," or "take." When God forgives us, he lifts his punishment and carries away our guilt.

Throughout the Scriptures, forgiveness follows confession. The book of James tells us to confess our sins to each other so that we might be healed (5:16). See, sin infects us, but God can heal us. First John encourages us to confess our sins because God is both faithful and just to forgive us *and* to cleanse us (1:9). When we confess our sins, God not only pardons us, he purifies us. Sin stains us with shame, but God can restore us.

1. When did you recently feel the weight of a sin? When did you feel the Lord lift that weight from you?

2. Who do you confess your sins to? How consistently?

FOUR

Hear This Word!

Amos 3:1–2 *Hear this word, people of Israel, the word the* Lord *has spoken against you—against the whole family I brought up out of Egypt:* ²*"You only have I chosen of all the families of the earth; therefore I will punish you for all your sins."*

Genesis 18:18–19 *"Abraham will surely become a great and powerful nation, and all nations on earth will be blessed through him.* ¹⁹*For I have chosen him, so that he will direct his children and his household after him to keep the way of the* Lord *by doing what is right and just, so that the* Lord *will bring about for Abraham what he has promised him."*

Key Observation. God graciously elects his people to advance his global mission.

Understanding the Word. Chapter 3 begins a new section in Amos. After the edicts against the nations (1:3–2:16), Amos delivers three judgment speeches—3:1–15, 4:1–13, and 5:1–17. Each speech starts with the summons "Hear this word." In 3:1, the Lord commands Israel to listen to the word he has spoken. Remember, this isn't Amos's word; it's the word the Lord has spoken against the people of Israel, or as Amos more poignantly puts it, against "you."

Interestingly, in the original language "against you the people of Israel" (literally "the sons of Israel") is followed by "against the *whole* family that I brought up from the land of Egypt." The initial phrase aims the Lord's word at the Northern Kingdom of Israel, but the second phrase expands the audience to include the Southern Kingdom of Judah. Whenever God speaks, all his people should listen. Even if the immediate implications are for Israel, Judah should heed the Lord's warnings. And so should we.

Before God issues his judgment, he references the exodus for a second time. He repeatedly reminds Israel that he is the God who saved them. His past acts frame everything he says. After this reminder, Amos uses two phrases loaded with meaning—"You only have I chosen" (literally "known") and "of all the families of the earth." These statements recall Israel's origins.

Israel traces its lineage back to Abram (a.k.a. Abraham). Israel began when the Lord called Abram in Genesis 12:1–3. God told Abram to leave everything —his country, his people, his family—and go to a new land. In return, God promised to make Abram into a great nation, to bless him, to make his name great, and to make him a blessing to *all the families of the earth*. The Lord reiterates these promises to Abram in several places, including Genesis 18:18–19. In that passage, God stated that he has chosen (again, literally "known") Abraham.

The verb "know" reinforces his personal relationship with Israel. They're his covenant people. He chose them out of all the families of the earth to be his. They're his "treasured possession" (e.g., Exod. 19:5). But he didn't select them solely for their sake. He elected them *from* the families of the earth *for* the families of the earth. He blessed Abraham's family in order to bless every family through them. Divine election comes with divine intentions and obligations. In order to be a blessing, Abraham and his offspring must "keep the way of the LORD by doing what is right and just" (Gen. 18:19).

Unfortunately, Israel fails to fulfill this calling. They've enjoyed the privileges of God's covenant but abandoned its requirements. Therefore, the Lord will punish Israel for her sins. Their election doesn't exempt them from judgment; it amplifies it.

The New Testament writers frequently apply the language of election to Jesus and the church. Paul says God chose the church to be set apart and without fault in Christ (Ephesians 1:4). Later he urges the Ephesian Christians "to live a life worthy of the calling you have received" (4:1). Like Israel, our gracious election in Jesus comes with both divine intentions *and* obligations.

1. Do you believe that God has divine intentions and expectations for you? Why or why not?

2. How are you being blessed? How are you blessing others?

FIVE

Divine Disaster

Amos 3:3–8 *Do two walk together unless they have agreed to do so? ⁴Does a lion roar in the thicket when it has no prey? Does it growl in its den when it has* *caught nothing? ⁵Does a bird swoop down to a trap on the ground when no bait is there? Does a trap spring up from the ground if it has not caught anything? ⁶When a trumpet sounds in a city, do not the people tremble? When disaster comes to a city, has not the Lord caused it?*

⁷Surely the Sovereign Lord does nothing without revealing his plan to his servants the prophets.

⁸The lion has roared—who will not fear? The Sovereign Lord has spoken—who can but prophesy?

Key Observation. God is constantly at work in the world to fulfill his purposes.

Understanding the Word. Having established why he'll punish Israel, God now reveals how he will do it. He discloses his punishment through a series of rhetorical questions. The first five are simple yes-or-no questions with implied negative answers. Each begins with a Hebrew letter that functions like a question mark. And each moves from an effect to its cause. Do people walk together unless they agreed to do so? No. Do lions roar without prey? No. Do they growl at nothing? No. Do birds dive unless they're enticed? No. Do traps spring without being sprung? No.

The sixth question suddenly breaks this pattern. If a city's warning trumpet is blown, won't its citizens tremble? This inquiry starts with "if" rather than the question marker. The cause also comes before the result and the answer is an implied positive. Yes! They'll be terrified! The change would have surprised Amos's listeners and highlighted the question. The change from hiking and hunting illustrations to battle imagery further intensifies the question.

This sets Israel up for the seventh and climatic question. This question also opens with "if," but returns to effect-cause pattern. If disaster comes upon a city, didn't the Lord do it? What's the answer? Is it yes like the last if question or no like the other effect-cause questions? The appropriate response is actually a tense and uncomfortable *yes*. When disaster strikes, God is the striker. Israel will be punished. Its cities will be destroyed. When this happens, the Lord will do it.

Verse 7 temporarily interrupts this inquiry to link the Lord's acts with his prophets. God not only acts in history; he speaks into it. He not only causes things to happen; he makes his plans known through his prophets. The two go together. God acts, and God speaks. His words make sense of his deeds. His prophets uncover the divine reasons for his actions.

The remaining rhetorical questions bolster this assertion. Both questions resume the cause-effect sequence of verse 6. But "who" replaces "if" and occurs in the middle of the progression. Notice the parallelism. "The lion has roared" parallels "the Sovereign Lord has spoken." "Who will not fear" parallels "who can but prophesy?" The answer is *no one*. When a lion roars, *no one* can resist fear. When God speaks, no prophet can stay silent.

After declaring that the Lord will discipline Israel (3:1) and disclosing how (3:6), the next two verses defend Amos's role in all of this (3:7–8). The prophet—like the trumpet—sounds the Lord's warning. He calls attention to what's going to happen, but he doesn't cause it. God does, so don't shoot the messenger!

In Amos, natural disasters have supernatural causes (4:6–11). This troubles many of us. Our discomfort reveals either a deistic worldview or a domesticated deity. For some of us, God is absent from the world. Everything that happens has only natural causes and scientific explanations—never divine ones. For others, God is tame. We've emphasized his goodness at the expense of his greatness—his love, grace, and mercy at the expense of his power, sovereignty, and holiness. But the Scriptures reveal a God who orchestrates history according to his purposes. This God is to be both loved and feared.

1. Have you distanced or domesticated God in the way you talk to or about him? How and why?

2. If God is constantly at work in the world, does this bolster or hinder your understanding of his goodness? Can you talk to God about that now?

WEEK TWO

GATHERING DISCUSSION OUTLINE

A. Open session in prayer.

B. View this week's video.

C. What general impressions and thoughts do you have after watching the video and reading the daily writings on these Scriptures? What, specifically, did this week's passages teach you about faith, life, and prayer?

D. Discuss selected questions from the daily readings. Always invite class members to share key insights or to raise questions that they found to be the most meaningful.

1. **KEY OBSERVATION:** We love God rightly when we treat others justly.

   DISCUSSION QUESTION: How do people with power and systems of justice treat the poor, oppressed, powerless, and needy in your city? How does the church treat them? How do you treat them?

2. **KEY OBSERVATION:** God expects his grace for us to evoke faithfulness from us.

   DISCUSSION QUESTION: How are you faithfully responding to God's grace during this season of your life?

3. **KEY OBSERVATION:** Only God can remove the burden of our guilt and lift the weight of his wrath.

   DISCUSSION QUESTION: When did you recently feel the weight of a sin? When did you feel the Lord lift that weight from you?

4. **KEY OBSERVATION:** God graciously elects his people to advance his global mission.

    DISCUSSION QUESTION: How are you being blessed? How are you blessing others?

5. **KEY OBSERVATION:** God is constantly at work in the world to fulfill his purposes.

    DISCUSSION QUESTION: Have you distanced or domesticated God in the way you talk to or about him? How and why?

E. Close session with prayer.

Amos 3–4

The Words of Amos: Part One

ONE

Severed and Shattered

Amos 3:9–12 ESV *Proclaim to the strongholds in Ashdod and to the strongholds in the land of Egypt, and say, "Assemble yourselves on the mountains of Samaria, and see the great tumults within her, and the oppressed in her midst."* *[10]"They do not know how to do right," declares the LORD, "those who store up violence and robbery in their strongholds."*

[11]Therefore thus says the Lord GOD: "An adversary shall surround the land and bring down your defenses from you, and your strongholds shall be plundered."

[12]Thus says the LORD: "As the shepherd rescues from the mouth of the lion two legs, or a piece of an ear, so shall the people of Israel who dwell in Samaria be rescued, with the corner of a couch and part of a bed."

Key Observation. At the heart of God's judgment, we find his justice and his mercy.

Understanding the Word. As the first judgment speech (3:1–15) continues, the Lord dispatches messengers to Israel's enemies—the Philistines (Ashdod) and Egyptians. They summon these nations' wealthiest people—those living in fortified palaces—to assemble on the mountains around Samaria. Samaria was the Northern Kingdom's capital at this time. From this spot, they could witness what was happening inside the city's walls. It's hard to imagine anything more humiliating for Israel than the Lord inviting rich heathens to see their sin.

Clearly, God's people have strayed from their calling to make him known to the nations. They have forfeited their privileged status and forsaken the ethical high ground. Instead of doing what's right, Israel's affluent stockpile their own fortresses through theft and violence. They've filled their pockets by inflicting pain and plundering the poor. Not even Israel's enemies treat their fellow citizens this cruelly.

Therefore, the Lord announces that an unidentified adversary will lay siege to Israel. He'll surround them and cut off their access to aid and any means of escape. He'll render them defenseless and then ransack Samaria. Israel's attacker will take by force what Israel's elite have taken the same way.

Historically speaking, this conquering force was the Assyrians. Shortly after Amos, one of history's best named tyrants, Tiglath-Pileser III, ascended Assyria's throne. He transformed his territories into a military superpower and led several campaigns against Israel and Judah. During the reign of Jeroboam II's successor, Pekah, the Assyrians conquered several Israelite cities. Then they conspired to assassinate Pekah and install Hoshea as king (2 Kings 15:29–30). Several years later, the next Assyrian leader, Shalmaneser V, invaded Israel and surrounded Samaria for three years. In 722, he conquered the capital and exiled its people. The Northern Kingdom never recovered.

But theologically speaking, their adversary was the Lord. He makes this clear in verse 6 and then dramatizes it in verse 12. Remember in Amos, the Lord is the lion—not the shepherd! After he attacks, only pieces remain. The shepherd can only rescue what remains of his sheep's carcass—dismembered legs and partial ears. These are the proofs of death—not the symbols of salvation (Exodus 22:10–13).

Scholars debate how to translate this passage's final phrases. At any rate, our interpretations must parallel the lion passage. The couch corner and bed part are not signs of hope; they are proof of destruction. When the Lord is finished, only shattered fragments of their lavish lifestyle will remain. In other words, no one will rescue Israel. They'll only recover broken pieces of furniture.

This is the first in a series of graphic portrayals of God's judgment. In Week One, we discussed how God's wrath unsettles us. And yet the idea of God ignoring injustice or standing idly by while people mistreat us or others *also* bothers us—and perhaps even more so. Naturally, we want God to be merciful when we have wronged others and vengeful when others have wronged us. But that's not how God operates. Instead, he is thoroughly committed to be merciful and just to everyone at all times. So, when we find ourselves troubled by Amos's depictions, we must remember those who need God's justice and consider how God displays mercy to those who have oppressed others.

1. When have you needed God to come to your aid because of others? When have others needed God to come to their aid because of you?

2. In each case, where did you see both God's mercy and his justice?

TWO

Fallen Houses

Amos 3:13–15 ESV *"Hear, and testify against the house of Jacob," declares the Lord GOD, the God of hosts, ¹⁴"that on the day I punish Israel for his transgressions, I will punish the altars of Bethel, and the horns of the altar shall be cut off and fall to the ground. ¹⁵I will strike the winter house along with the summer house, and the houses of ivory shall perish, and the great houses shall come to an end," declares the LORD.*

Key Observation. We must make the Lord the foundation of our lives or everything crumbles.

Understanding the Word. First, the Lord invites Israel's enemies to observe her transgressions (3:9). Now he calls those nations to testify to what they've seen. As God makes his case, he suddenly refers to Israel as the house of Jacob. Why? Did he forget their name or does this name mean something?

Jacob was Abraham's grandson. He earned his name by clutching his twin brother Esau's heel during birth (Genesis 25:19–28). Grabbing someone's heel is like going behind someone's back. He lived up to his name when he deceived his father, stole his brother's blessing, and then skipped town (Genesis 27). Years later, Jacob and Esau reconciled. The night before they reunited, Jacob wrestled with God, and God changed his name to Israel—one who has struggled with God (Genesis 32:22–32). His new name symbolized his new identity. The Lord uses their old name because they have returned to Jacob's old ways.

As Israel's trial continues, God directly addresses the accused rather than questioning his witnesses. Then he discloses himself as the adversary of verse 11 and declares that he will punish Israel. God launches his campaign in Bethel. Centuries earlier, Jacob spent the night in this place. While he was sleeping, the Lord revealed himself to Jacob in a dream. When Jacob woke up, he named it "Bethel" or, "the house of God." But the house of God now houses one of Jeroboam's golden calves, so God decides to retaliate.

Why would the Lord cut the horns off Bethel's altar? In and around Israel, people worshipped by sacrificing animals on altars. Jeroboam probably patterned his altars after the tabernacle's—Israel's pre-temple worship tent (Exodus 27:1–8). The square altar would've had horns sticking out of its top corners. Priests would apply blood to these horns during certain offerings (Exodus 29:12; Leviticus 4). They would also dab blood on them to purify the altar (Exodus 30:10; Leviticus 8:14–24; 16:18). Fugitives fearing retribution for their crimes would seek sanctuary by grasping an altar's horns (Exodus 21:12–14; 1 Kings 1:50–51; 2:28). By removing them, God forcibly retires the altar and reclaims his house.

Then in verse 15 the Lord comes back to the homes of the wealthy. It turns out they have seasonal houses, and they've furnished both with ivory. This is just another indication that they live in abundance while others live in lack. For this reason, the Lord will shatter these shelters. Their great houses will end. "Great" can and should be translated as "many." The house of God (Bethel), the houses of the well-to-do, *and* the house of Jacob will all end. Israel built upon the faulty foundations of godlessness and greed and, as a result, all their houses will crumble.

Similarly, Jesus taught his followers that those who obey his teachings build their lives on steadfast stone, but those who ignore his words build on unstable sand (Matthew 7:24–27). Jesus also told Peter that he would build his entire church on the revelation that he is "the Christ, the Son of the living God" (Matt. 16:16–18 ESV). He calls us to align our lives on this foundation. We have God as the center, or we have nothing at all.

1. What houses need to be toppled in your life? In your church? In your city? In our world?

2. Is there an area of your life that you feel is falling apart? How could God be inviting you to build a different foundation?

THREE
Women, Wealth, and Worship

Amos 4:1–3 ESV *"Hear this word, you cows of Bashan, who are on the mountain of Samaria, who oppress the poor, who crush the needy, who say to your husbands, 'Bring, that we may drink!' ²The Lord God has sworn by his holiness that, behold, the days are coming upon you, when they shall take you away with hooks, even the last of you with fishhooks. ³And you shall go out through the breaches, each one straight ahead; and you shall be cast out into Harmon," declares the Lord.*

Key Observation. Who we worship is most clearly displayed in how we use money.

Understanding the Word. Chapter 4 contains Amos's second judgment speech. It characteristically beckons "Hear this word." This time the Lord addresses the "cows of Bashan." Occasionally, the Old Testament writers lovingly compared women to certain animals (Song of Solomon 4). This isn't one of those times!

Bashan was a lush region northeast of the sea of Galilee. The Scriptures praised the area's agricultural production. Deuteronomy noted its portly lambs and rams (32:14). The psalmist marveled at its hearty bulls (22:12). Ezekiel imagined a feast of its beasts (39:18). Bashan's cows ate well, and it showed. Apparently, so did Israel's upper-class housewives. Now the Lord is calling them to account for their excess.

The Lord accuses Israel's wealthy women of three egregious acts. The first two echo his initial allegations against the kingdom (2:6–7). They've exploited the poor and mistreated the needy. They've plumped themselves up by pushing others down. The third charge pertains to their relationship with their husbands, or literally "lords." (This word may suggest that not all the women are wives.) These women made incessant demands. Their insatiable thirst for more drove their men to act unjustly and fund their luxurious lifestyles.

Therefore, the Lord vows by his holiness to punish them. His holiness distinguishes him from all other gods (Exodus 15:11). He is radically uncommon and unlike any other. The psalmist connects this same holiness pledge to the promise God made to David and his pact not to lie (Psalm 89:35). In other words, the Lord means what he says and does what he says.

The statements following God's pledge detail what will happen to Israel's leading ladies when the Assyrian army breaches the city. The Assyrians perfected several gruesome tactics to terrify and suppress their enemies, including human impalement and forced migration. This passage reflects those historical realities. When the Assyrians arrive, they will slaughter these women and hang their bodies on meat hooks and harpoons. Then, one after another, they'll carry their corpses through the broken walls and away from their land. Then they'll cast them aside in Harmon (see Joshua 8:29; 10:27; 2 Samuel 18:17; 2 Kings 9:30–37; 13:21; Jeremiah 41:9). The exact location of Harmon is unknown, but it may be a reference to Mount Hermon—the highest mountain in the range northeast of Israel (Amos 5:27). This graphic imagery indicates total annihilation or permanent exile. Either way, the life Israel enjoys will end.

Beyond describing the physical appearance of Israel's mistresses, Amos's imagery may also relate to the worship of Jeroboam's golden calves. The women may have adopted the beliefs and customs of ancient pagan religions and seen themselves as God's companions. If so, then the Lord once again condemns Israel's upper class for both their financial and their spiritual practices.

The Bible frequently connects worship and money. According to Jesus, no one can serve God and money (Luke 16:13). You may try, but when the rubber meets the road, you can only be exclusively loyal to one. Israel's elite pledged their allegiance to economic excess, and it showed up in their relationships with God and others. Likewise, how we view and use money ultimately reveals who or what we worship.

1. In what ways have the teachings of the Bible shaped your view and use of money?

2. How do Amos's teachings about money and excess challenge your perspectives or practices?

FOUR

Come! Let's Sin Together!

Amos 4:4–5 ESV *"Come to Bethel, and transgress; to Gilgal, and multiply transgression; bring your sacrifices every morning, your tithes every three days; 5offer a sacrifice of thanksgiving of that which is leavened, and proclaim freewill offerings, publish them; for so you love to do, O people of Israel!" declares the Lord God.*

Key Observation. The Lord desires our private affections over our public performances.

Understanding the Word. "Come to Bethel!" "Come to Gilgal!"—Amos stands outside the sanctuary in Bethel (see 7:10–14) and invites people to worship there or in Gilgal. This is the first time Amos mentions Gilgal. When Israel first entered the promised land, they encamped at Gilgal (Joshua 3–5), and the prophet Samuel anointed their first king Saul there (1 Samuel 11:14–15). Though it wasn't one of Jeroboam's worship centers, Israel apparently offered sacrifices there in the eighth century (Hosea 12:11). Amos pays Gilgal considerably more attention than Jeroboam's other worship center—Dan. He names Gilgal in 4:4 and twice in 5:5, but he only mentions Dan once (8:14). Neither comes close to Bethel, which gets most of Amos's ire.

"Come to Bethel and sin!" "Come to Gilgal and sin even more!" The text literally reads, "Come and rebel!" and "Come and increase your rebellion!" Can you imagine someone inviting you to church this way? "Come sin with us this Sunday." Or a worship leader inviting a congregation to stand and sin together? Amos uses a popular call to worship to mock Bethel's worshippers (Psalm 95). The Lord's prophets frequently insulted their opponents. Yes, they trash-talked in the Bible.

The Hebrew word for "worship" pictures someone bowing down before a superior to pledge his/her allegiance. At its core, worship should express both love and loyalty to the Lord. But rather than demonstrating their fidelity, Israel feigns devotion for selfish gain. Through Amos, the Lord unmasks what really motivates their worship.

Israel offers their sacrifices for the morning and their tithes for three days. "Every" is not in the original language, but the time references imply religious repetition. The morning "sacrifices" were likely the peace offerings detailed in Leviticus 3:1–17, 7:11–36, and 22:17–33. These included provisions for a leavened offering of thanksgiving (7:12–15; 22:29–30) and freewill offerings (7:16–17; 22:18–23). The "tithes" represented one-tenth of the land's produce (Leviticus 27:30; Deuteronomy 14:22–27). The Lord prescribed all of these offerings. In this way, Israel's worship appears both prompt and proper.

But Israel's problem lies within. They do the right things for the wrong reasons. They announce their voluntary offerings. They post their gifts to draw attention to themselves. This is what they really love. They prize public recognition more than the Lord. They want to showcase their wealth, not surrender their lives to the Lord. Subsequently God refuses their sacrifices. "These are *your* sacrifices and *your* tithes, not *mine*! They are expressions of your rebellion, not your devotion."

Jesus agrees with Amos's assessment in Matthew 6:1–6. He instructs his disciples not to be like the hypocrites who publicize their charity and their prayers. They pretend to praise the Lord, but they really seek the praise of others. They want human commendations more than they want a relationship with God. Jesus says if that's who and what they want, that's who and what they'll get. Their motives reveal their true lord and their desired reward. And so do ours.

1. How might this text shape or challenge your church's public worship gatherings?

2. What is something right that you do for the wrong reasons? Can you ask God now to fill your heart with the right intention?

FIVE

Persistent Pursuit

Amos 4:6–11 ESV *"I gave you cleanness of teeth in all your cities, and lack of bread in all your places, yet you did not return to me," declares the* LORD.

⁷"I also withheld the rain from you when there were yet three months to the harvest; I would send rain on one city, and send no rain on another city; one field would have rain, and the field on which it did not rain would wither; ⁸so two or three cities would wander to another city to drink water, and would not be satisfied; yet you did not return to me," declares the LORD.

⁹"I struck you with blight and mildew; your many gardens and your vineyards, your fig trees and your olive trees the locust devoured; yet you did not return to me," declares the LORD.

¹⁰"I sent among you a pestilence after the manner of Egypt; I killed your young men with the sword, and carried away your horses, and I made the stench of your camp go up into your nostrils; yet you did not return to me," declares the LORD.

¹¹"I overthrew some of you, as when God overthrew Sodom and Gomorrah, and you were as a brand plucked out of the burning; yet you did not return to me," declares the LORD.

Key Observation. The Lord displays his love to us through his kindness *and* through his discipline.

Understanding the Word. Today's passage continues Amos's assertion that some natural disasters have supernatural causes (see Week Two, Day Five). It also adds to the idea by articulating the aims of the Lord's acts. God uses famine (v. 6), drought (vv. 7–8), crop diseases (v. 9), agricultural pests (v. 9), plagues (v. 10), military defeat (v. 10), and other disasters (v. 11) for his purposes. In Amos, they're the very things God did to get Israel's attention before he sent the prophet. (They're also the very things God threatened to use in Leviticus 26:14–33 and Deuteronomy 28:15–68 if Israel broke his laws.)

He cleaned their teeth by withholding bread, and he held back the rain their crops desperately needed. When he did open the skies, the rain fell erratically. He sent rain on a city or a field but not on those nearby. This forced Israel to roam around looking for a drink but unable to quench their thirst. He left them without bread and water—the very things he had faithfully provided them in the wilderness.

Then when Israel managed to grow a crop, God struck their fields with blight and mildew. A scorching east wind burned their grain before they could gather it, and a devastating disease infected the rest. After that, he commissioned locusts to consume their gardens, vineyards, and orchards. (Remember Amos had his own trees, so he understood the severity of these words; Amos 7:14.)

The Lord even treated his people like he did the Egyptians (Exodus 9:3). They suffered through some of the same signs as those who had enslaved them. But this time they were on the receiving end of God's reproof. He sent Israel pestilence and sword. Her citizens died from plague and her future fathers from fatal wounds. So many people died that their army encampments reeked of decomposing bodies. Still no one could escape the smell because their enemies had stolen their horses.

Finally, he overthrew some of their cities just as he had done to Sodom and Gomorrah. The Lord wiped out those places by raining fire on them (Genesis 19). Subsequently, they became the Bible's go-to example of divine annihilation. Nearly all of their inhabitants died. Only Abraham's nephew and his daughters survived. Likewise, the Lord had previously saved some of Amos's audience.

Amos organizes these seven judgment signs into five sets. With each set, Israel's afflictions worsen. They progress from famine to the ancient equivalent of Hiroshima. Each set concludes with the same declaration—"yet you did not return to me." The Lord repeats this clause *five* times. He wants his people to repent. He longs for them to turn away from evil and back to him. And he does everything he can.

The Lord repeatedly graces them, but they continually turn away (Amos 2:9–11). So, he regularly disciplines them, but time and again they refuse to come back. Both his kindness and his rebuke are expressions of his love and evidence of his desire for a relationship with them and with us. We rarely think of God's discipline this positively, but the writer of Hebrews reminds us, "The Lord disciplines the one he loves" (12:6 ESV). He goes on to demonstrate how a parent's correction actually proves they love their kids (vv. 7–11). The same is true for God.

1. When has God's kindness led you to repentance?

2. When have you sensed God's discipline in your life? What did you think about him during that time? How did you respond to his correction?

WEEK THREE

GATHERING DISCUSSION OUTLINE

A. Open session in prayer.

B. View this week's video.

C. What general impressions and thoughts do you have after watching the video and reading the daily writings on these Scriptures? What, specifically, did this week's passages teach you about faith, life, and prayer?

D. Discuss selected questions from the daily readings. Always invite class members to share key insights or to raise questions that they found to be the most meaningful.

1. **KEY OBSERVATION:** At the heart of God's judgment, we find his justice and his mercy.

   DISCUSSION QUESTION: When have you needed God to come to your aid because of others? When have others needed God to come to their aid because of you?

2. **KEY OBSERVATION:** We must make the Lord the foundation of our lives or everything crumbles.

   DISCUSSION QUESTION: Is there an area of your life that you feel is falling apart? How could God be inviting you to build a different foundation?

3. **KEY OBSERVATION:** Who we worship is most clearly displayed in how we use money.

DISCUSSION QUESTION: How do Amos's teachings about money and excess challenge your perspectives or practices?

4. **KEY OBSERVATION:** The Lord desires our private affections over our public performances.

   DISCUSSION QUESTION: How might this text shape or challenge your church's public worship gatherings?

5. **KEY OBSERVATION:** The Lord displays his love to us through his kindness *and* through his discipline.

   DISCUSSION QUESTION: When have you sensed God's discipline in your life? What did you think about him during that time? How did you respond to his correction?

E. Close session with prayer.

Amos 4–5

The Words of Amos: Part Two

ONE

Brace Yourself

Amos 4:12–13 NRSV *Therefore thus I will do to you, O Israel; because I will do this to you, prepare to meet your God, O Israel!*

¹³For lo, the one who forms the mountains, creates the wind, reveals his thoughts to mortals, makes the morning darkness, and treads on the heights of the earth—the LORD, the God of hosts, is his name!

Key Observation. The Scriptures encourage us to always be prepared to meet God.

Understanding the Word. "*Thus* I will do . . . because I will do *this*." In these verses, God commits to take action against Israel. But what exactly is he going to do? The words "thus" and "this" point back to the verb "return" in verse 11. After Israel repeatedly refuses to "return" to God through repentance, the Lord decides to "return" to them in judgment.

The language in verse 12 reminds Israel of its post-exodus encounter with God at Mount Sinai (Exodus 19:9–25). Through Moses, the Lord had told Israel to prepare for him to visit. Three days later, God descended on the mountain in fire. Thunder, lightning, a thick cloud, trumpet blasts, and smoke followed him. He made Sinai quake and his people tremble. Then "Moses brought the people out of the camp to *meet* God" (v. 17 NRSV, italics added).

The Lord came down on Sinai to make a covenant with Israel (Exodus 19:3–5; 20:1–17). A covenant was an ancient political treaty. It bound two parties together in a family-like relationship. The purpose of his visit was gracious, but his presence was terrifying and even dangerous. Moses actually warned Israel to keep their distance or die (Exodus 19:22).

In Amos, God vows to come back for a different reason. He plans to pay Israel a visit to repay them for breaking his covenant and refusing to change their ways. When Moses announced God's pending arrival, he advised them *how* to get ready (Exodus 19:9–15). But Amos tells them *who* to get ready for.

He is the God who shapes the mountains and authors the wind. He divulges his plans to his prophets (Week Two, Day Five). He turns the dawn into darkness. He tramples on the earth's high places. In other words, he judges unorthodox worship centers like Bethel and Gilgal (Week One, Day Five). He is the God of hosts.

Amos uses the designation "the God of hosts" often (3:13; 5:14–16, 27; 6:8, 14; 9:5). He's not alone; other Old Testament writers also describe God this way. "Hosts" refer to armies, so God is a commander in chief. At times, God and his armies fight on Israel's behalf (e.g., 1 Samuel 15:2). But this time, they are marching against the Northern Kingdom.

This command to prepare for the arrival of the all-creating, self-revealing, cosmic-judging, and army-leading God concludes Amos's second judgment speech. Israel's leading ladies are oppressing the poor, crushing the needy, and compelling their husbands to join them (4:1–3). Israel's sacrifices are expressions of self-promoting rebellion, not self-sacrificing faith (4:4–5). Israel's resistance to the Lord's correctives is unrelenting (4:6–11). Therefore, Israel must prepare to meet their Maker.

In the New Testament, God sent John the Baptist to prepare people for another visit (Mark 1:2–3). Later, Jesus announced that God's kingdom had arrived (Mark 1:14–15). It actually arrived when he did! Before his death, resurrection, and ascension, Jesus instructed his followers to always be prepared for the kingdom to fully arrive when he comes again (e.g., Matthew 25). We don't know when this will happen, but living with this end in mind is truly the wisest way to live.

1. Which image of God—Creator, Revealer, Judge, or Commander—comforts you? Which challenges you? Why?

2. How can you live today with the end in mind?

TWO

The God Who Grieves

Amos 5:1–7 NRSV *Hear this word that I take up over you in lamentation, O house of Israel: ²Fallen, no more to rise, is maiden Israel; forsaken on her land, with no one to raise her up.*

³For thus says the Lord God: The city that marched out a thousand shall have a hundred left, and that which marched out a hundred shall have ten left.

⁴For thus says the Lord to the house of Israel: Seek me and live; ⁵but do not seek Bethel, and do not enter into Gilgal or cross over to Beer-sheba; for Gilgal shall surely go into exile, and Bethel shall come to nothing.

⁶Seek the Lord and live, or he will break out against the house of Joseph like fire, and it will devour Bethel, with no one to quench it. ⁷Ah, you that turn justice to wormwood, and bring righteousness to the ground!

Key Observation. While he judges, God grieves.

Understanding the Word. Amos's third judgment speech (5:1–17) depicts the Lord presiding over Israel's funeral. He laments the inevitable loss of his beloved. He's not indifferent or delighted; he's grieved. God doesn't judge with a smile on his face but with tears in his eyes. To him, Israel is a young woman whose life ended prematurely. She died helpless and alone, and the Lord mourns.

According to verse 3, Israel died in battle. One of her cities sent a thousand troops into war, but only a hundred survived. Another committed a hundred soldiers and lost ninety. Her decimated armies signal her total defeat and the death of the nation.

The next few verses seem out of place; therefore, scholars debate how to read them. They may indicate there's hope for Israel. God has written their obituary, but they're not dead yet. If Israel will seek the Lord, they'll live. If they'll come to him instead of Bethel, Gilgal, and Beer-sheba, he'll spare them. (Beer-sheba was a city in southern Judah associated with Abraham [Genesis 21:14–33; 22:19], Isaac [26:23–33], and Jacob [46:1–4]. It remained a place of pilgrimage for Israel after they separated from Judah.)

On the other hand, these verses may encourage Israel to seek refuge in Judah. God has doomed Israel and its sanctuaries. He'll exile Gilgal and destroy Bethel because they're in Israel (5:5). But he'll seemingly spare Beer-sheba because it's in Judah. Therefore, if Israel will seek God in Judah's temple, they'll survive.

However, in light of the funeral context, these verses more likely repeat things God previously said to them. He implored Israel to seek him, but they didn't. This parallels Amos 4:6–13, where the Lord regularly disciplined Israel, but they didn't return to him. Because they continually spurn him, the Lord will censure the house of Joseph, which is another name for Israel. (Joseph was one of Jacob's sons. Israel's largest tribes descended from his sons Ephraim and Manasseh. Joseph was also the first exile to Egypt, which may explain the use of his name here.)

Verse 7 can also be confusing. Our English translations obscure who specifically turns justice into wormwood and brings righteousness to the ground (5:7). In the original language, it's clearly Bethel. The Lord will devour its inhabitants because they turn justice into a bitter-tasting plant. They pervert justice by denying it to the poor (Exodus 23:6). They make something sweet foul. They throw righteousness to the ground and discarded what the Lord desired (Genesis 18:19).

The Bible frequently pairs justice and righteousness. The first time they're tied together is in Genesis 18:19. The Lord chose Abraham and his offspring "to keep the way of the Lord by doing righteousness and justice" (Week Two, Day Four). But by Amos's day, they had forsaken their foundation, and their founder now weeps at their funeral.

God is the God who grieves. We see this clearly in Jesus. He wept over Lazarus (John 11:35). And in a passage similar to Amos, he shed tears as he judged Jerusalem (Luke 19:41–44). Rather than rejoicing in or remaining unaffected by our sin and its consequences, God's heart aches even as he acts to make things right.

1. Why would Israel ignore God's pleas? Why might you?

2. Why is God's grief significant? What does this image tell you about God's character?

THREE

His Name Is Yahweh

Amos 5:8–9 NRSV *The one who made the Pleiades and Orion, and turns deep darkness into the morning, and darkens the day into night, who calls for the waters of the sea, and pours them out on the surface of the earth, the LORD is his name, ⁹who makes destruction flash out against the strong, so that destruction comes upon the fortress.*

Key Observation. God's name reveals his character and reminds us what he can do.

Understanding the Word. As the Lord's lament continues, he contrasts Israel's acts with his own. He reminds Israel who he is and what he does. As he did in Amos 4:12–13, he calls their attention to his rule over creation and his name. His proclamation demonstrates that if they had sought him—if they had returned to him—he had the power to revive them.

They may transform justice to wormwood and toss righteousness to the earth, but he forms and even transforms the heavens. He set the constellations in the skies (Job 9:9; 38:31). He can turn the blackest night into morning light or the daylight into darkness. He spoke light into the darkness and created time itself (Genesis 1:3–5). He set the lights in the sky to rule the night and day (Genesis 1:14–19). He shrouded Egypt for three days but let the sun shine on his people (Exodus 10:21–23). He tamed the deep, collected the waters, and named them seas (Genesis 1:2, 6–10). He alone can unleash the waters as he did in the days of Noah (Genesis 6–8). But his power isn't limited to the cosmos. He can also devastate the strongest person and the mightiest fortress with a lightning flash.

In the middle of this powerful proclamation, Amos declares "the LORD is his name." The prophet used this phrase in 4:13 and he'll use it again in 9:6. You may have noticed that throughout the Old Testament "LORD" often appears in small caps. This is how most English Bibles translate God's personal name.

God first revealed his name when he spoke to Moses from a burning bush and enlisted him to lead Israel out of Egypt (Exodus 3). Moses responded to this commission with a couple of questions. "Why me? And if the Israelites ask me, who are you?" (vv. 11–13). God replied, "I AM WHO I AM" (3:14). In Hebrew, the third person form—"HE IS"—is spelled with four letters which correspond to YHWH in English.

We think this name would've been pronounced "Yahweh," but we're not 100 percent sure. Our uncertainty is partially related to the third commandment, which instructed Israel not to misuse this name. Jews historically observed this command by not pronouncing God's name at all. Instead, whenever they came across YHWH in the Scriptures, they read "Adonai," which means "Lord." This is why our translations use "the LORD."

The commandment literally prohibited Israel from "carrying" God's name in an unworthy manner. In other words, Israel should not do or say anything in God's name that would misrepresent him. In the ancient world, a person's name was synonymous with his or her character. Correspondingly, the Lord's name represents him. The Old Testament associates his name with creation, revelation, salvation, and presence. He's the God who made everything and made himself known. He's also the God who saved and lived with his people.

This is still who God is! When God revealed himself through his Son, he gave him two names—Jesus and Emmanuel. His name is Jesus because he saves us from sin (Matthew 1:21). His name is Emmanuel because "he is God with us" (Matthew 1:23). HE IS WHO HE IS!

1. Spend a few minutes contemplating the power of God in creation. Which aspects most remind you of his strength and ability?

2. How are you using God's name in your speech and acts? What would need to change today for you to better represent him?

FOUR

Corrupt Courts

Amos 5:10–13 NRSV *They hate the one who reproves in the gate, and they abhor the one who speaks the truth. ¹¹Therefore because you trample on the poor and take from them levies of grain, you have built houses of hewn stone, but you shall not live in them; you have planted pleasant vineyards, but you shall not drink their wine. ¹²For I know how many are your transgressions, and how great* *are your sins—you who afflict the righteous, who take a bribe, and push aside the needy in the gate.* *[13]Therefore the prudent will keep silent in such a time; for it is an evil time.*

Key Observation. God commissions us to establish justice for everyone and particularly the poor.

Understanding the Word. Eulogies normally highlight the praiseworthy aspects of someone's life even if there isn't much to praise. But the Lord's speech spotlights Israel's unscrupulous sides. He previously denounced her sanctuaries (5:4–7). Now he reprimands her courts. Israel's courts literally met inside of each city's gate, which served as entry points and public meeting spaces. These fortified structures contained several side rooms. The local male elders would meet in these areas to settle disputes, sustain law, and secure justice for all.

The Lord gave Israel's elders explicit instructions to ensure the court's integrity. For example, he barred witnesses from falsifying their testimonies (Exodus 20:16; Deuteronomy 5:20). Israel permitted capital punishment, so lying on the stand could lead to death. To prevent perjury from happening, the elders needed multiple witnesses to convict someone (Deuteronomy 17:6–7; 19:15). The Lord also mandated that Israel's elders investigate every accusation. If they determined someone committed perjury, he/she faced the same punishment as the accused (Deuteronomy 19:15–20).

Elsewhere, God prohibited Israel's elders from denying justice to the poor and accepting bribes from the rich (e.g., Exodus 23:1–9; Leviticus 19:11–18; Deuteronomy 16:18–20). Those charged with maintaining justice must not be coerced by the wealthy. If they cave, the whole system will collapse, and it will fall on those without means and not those with it.

Some of Israel's elders were just. But Israel's mob bosses scorned them for opposing their business practices. They had prospered by unfairly taxing Israel's peasant farmers. ("Trample" probably refers to another kind of grain levy.) They used some of their earnings to construct houses from expensive stones like those adorning Solomon's temple (1 Kings 5:17). They spent the rest on choice vineyards. To preserve their lifestyle, the rich ostracized the righteous, exchanged bribes, and kept the poor from pursuing litigation. They so thoroughly debased the system that silence became the wisest course of action.

Through Amos, the Lord condemns Israel's elite and sentences them to exile. They'll no longer inhabit their mansions or enjoy the fruit of their vines. They've forfeited their rights to the land by refusing to follow the Lord's decrees. Consequently, he'll banish them from the land, which is tantamount to death.

Today's verses recall the Lord's original indictment of Israel, particularly their maltreatment of the poor (Amos 2:4–6). However, God's concern for the poor is not limited to Israel or the Old Testament. God anointed Jesus to bring good news to the poor (Luke 4:18). Jesus encouraged his followers to welcome them at our tables (14:7–24). Those who accepted Jesus evidenced their faith in him by giving to the needy (Luke 19:1–10). When the early church recognized Paul's ministry to the Gentiles, they requested he remember the poor (Galatians 2:10).

Some scholars have suggested that God prefers the poor and commands us to as well. At the very least, God wants us to keep them in mind. The poor are often forgotten, more often ignored, and too often despised and oppressed. But God calls us to be partial to rather than prejudiced against those in need. We do so not only by providing for them but also by protecting them from injustice.

1. In what ways do you prefer those with means over those without means?

2. How do you or can you remember the poor in your neighborhood, city, or state?

FIVE

Seeking Good

Amos 5:14–17 NRSV *Seek good and not evil, that you may live; and so the* L*ORD*, *the God of hosts, will be with you, just as you have said.* *[15]Hate evil and love good, and establish justice in the gate; it may be that the* L*ORD*, *the God of hosts, will be gracious to the remnant of Joseph.*

[16]Therefore thus says the L*ORD*, *the God of hosts, the Lord: In all the squares there shall be wailing; and in all the streets they shall say, "Alas! alas!" They shall*

call the farmers to mourning, and those skilled in lamentation, to wailing; ¹⁷in all the vineyards there shall be wailing, for I will pass through the midst of you, says the LORD.

Key Observation. We seek God by seeking good.

Understanding the Word. Before Amos arrived, the Lord implored Israel to seek him and live (Amos 5:4–6). We noted that on their own those verses could sound optimistic. But then they wouldn't fit with the rest of the passage. When we read them as a eulogy, we realize they recount messages and opportunities that Israel ignored.

In today's reading, God instructs Israel to seek good that they may live. Again, the tone of the first two verses seems surprisingly hopeful. But the literary setting still suggests otherwise. *If* Israel had sought good and not evil, *then* God and his armies would have been with them and graciously preserved a remnant of them. But as we saw in the previous verses, they did the opposite. It's likely, given the inclusion "just as you have said" that Israel presumed God's presence and favor. They assumed they were good with God whether they did good or not.

But God and good are intimately related. Whereas Amos 5:6 charges Israel to seek God and live, Amos 5:14 charges them (and us) to seek good and live. God and good are used interchangeably. To seek good *is* to seek God. Why? Because God *is* good (e.g., Psalms 34:8; 100:5; 135:3; 145:9; Mark 10:18). Therefore, his people worship him and represent him by doing good and putting his character on display. Sadly, Israel set righteousness down in the sanctuary (5:7) and failed to set justice up in the gates (5:15).

The final verses of this speech end where it began—with lamentation (vv. 1–2). This section repeats "wailing" three times and "woe" (or "alas") twice to intensify the funeral scene. The corruption of the city's court distresses the city's streets and squares. The overtaxed farmers join those who know how to mourn. Their mourning spills out of the gate into the very vineyards Israel's elite gained improperly.

What's the reason for all this grieving? "For I will pass through the midst of you." Israel knew what this meant. In Exodus 12, the Lord *passed through* Egypt and struck down the firstborn son in every Egyptian household. However, he instructed the Israelites to smear lamb's blood on their doorways. Then when he saw the blood, he *passed over* their homes, spared their lives, and brought the house of Joseph out of Egypt. They weep because the Lord who once *passed over* them will now *pass through* them. He *passed over* them to save them; he'll *pass through* them to judge them. He rescued them so that they could do good; he'll revisit them to judge them for not doing it.

In his letter to the Ephesians, Paul writes that God saves us by his good grace and not by our good deeds. But he goes on to say that God made us to do good in Jesus (Ephesians 2:8–10). Once again, God's grace and good works go together. Jesus' own brother James insists that "faith by itself, if it has no works, is dead" (James 2:17). Because God is good, those who trust God seek good. God and good are inseparable. So, let's have both. Let's love God *and* love what's good for God *is* good.

1. What good has God designed you to do in Jesus?

2. Have you done all the good you can and avoided all the evil you can?

WEEK FOUR

GATHERING DISCUSSION OUTLINE

A. Open session in prayer.

B. View this week's video.

C. What general impressions and thoughts do you have after watching the video and reading the daily writings on these Scriptures? What, specifically, did this week's passages teach you about faith, life, and prayer?

D. Discuss selected questions from the daily readings. Always invite class members to share key insights or to raise questions that they found to be the most meaningful.

   1. **KEY OBSERVATION:** The Scriptures encourage us to always be prepared to meet God.

   DISCUSSION QUESTION: Which image of God—Creator, Revealer, Judge, or Commander—comforts you? Which challenges you? Why?

   2. **KEY OBSERVATION:** While he judges, God grieves.

   DISCUSSION QUESTION: Why is God's grief significant? What does this image tell you about God's character?

   3. **KEY OBSERVATION:** God's name reveals his character and reminds us what he can do.

   DISCUSSION QUESTION: How are you using God's name in your speech and acts? What would need to change today for you to better represent him?

4. **KEY OBSERVATION:** God commissions us to establish justice for everyone and particularly the poor.

    DISCUSSION QUESTION: In what ways do you prefer those with means over those without means?

5. **KEY OBSERVATION:** We seek God by seeking good.

    DISCUSSION QUESTION: Have you done all the good you can and avoided all the evil you can?

E. Close session with prayer.

Amos 5–6

The Woes of Amos

ONE

The Day of the Lord

Amos 5:18–20 *Woe to you who long for the day of the LORD! Why do you long for the day of the LORD? That day will be darkness, not light. ¹⁹It will be as though a man fled from a lion only to meet a bear, as though he entered his house and rested his hand on the wall only to have a snake bite him. ²⁰Will not the day of the LORD be darkness, not light—pitch-dark, without a ray of brightness?*

Key Observation. Our confidence in the Lord's return should provoke us to faithful love.

Understanding the Word. Today's passage begins the fourth division in Amos. After delivering three judgment speeches (3:1–5:17), Amos now issues two woe oracles (5:18–27; 6:1–14). The word "woe" occurs more than fifty times in the Old Testament, mostly in the prophets. It typically sounds a foreboding tone. Before Amos, no one associated "woe" with the day of the Lord.

This "day" originated in Israel's history with God. Israel believed God was a divine warrior who fought their battles. We hear this after the exodus as the Israelites sing, "The LORD is a warrior; the LORD is his name" (Exod. 15:3). We hear it again in Moses' prayer in the wilderness, "Rise up, LORD! May your enemies be scattered; may your foes flee before you" (Num. 10:35). We see it when Israel marches around Jericho, and God topples the city's walls (Joshua 6:1–21). We see it again as the Lord rains hail about Israel's enemies

(Joshua 10:9–11) and gives them victory over the Philistines and the Amalekites (1 Samuel 7:10; 15:2; 2 Samuel 5:17–19).

These experiences and several others understandably led Israel to believe that God was always on their side. After a while, they even began to hope that another day would come when the Lord would grant them total triumph. For example, Isaiah spoke about a day of vengeance when the Lord would destroy all of Israel's enemies (Isaiah 34). According to Amos, Israel's confidence in the day of the Lord developed into an intense longing for it to come (5:18). Amos uses the same verb for longing that God condemned in the tenth commandment—"Do not covet" (Exod. 20:17; Deut. 5:21). The verb choice suggests that Israel wants the wrong thing.

Amos then utilizes a couple of questions to rattle their optimism in and subvert their expectations for the day of the Lord. He insists that day will bring darkness not light—retribution not rescue. Like the person who escaped a lion only to encounter a bear, or when resting at home, was bitten by a snake, Israel may have dodged death but an unpleasant surprise waits for them at home. They shouldn't mistake the Lord's past grace as a future guarantee. Because they've switched sides and turned against God, their fortunes will be reversed.

Amos reimagines the day of the Lord as a day of judgment rather than salvation. Several other prophets follow his lead. Jesus and the New Testament writers mostly do as well. They continue the theme of unexpected doom (Luke 10:8–12; 2 Thessalonians 1:5–10). Yet they also reintroduce hope, specifically the hope of resurrection and new creation (John 6:39–40; 2 Peter 3:11–13). For them, the day of the Lord is a day of judgment and salvation.

Subsequently, the New Testament cautions us not to naively believe that *God* is always on *our* side. Instead, it calls *us* to join *God's* side, so that when Jesus returns we may receive a reward for our good works rather than a rebuke for our unjust acts (1 Corinthians 3:11–15). Therefore, as we see the future coming, "Let us consider how we may spur one another on toward love and good deeds" (Heb. 10:24).

1. When you think about Jesus, do you expect doom, rescue, or both? How does this shape your prayers and your decisions?

2. Who inspires you to faithful love? How?

T W O

Repulsive Worship

Amos 5:21–27 *"I hate, I despise your religious festivals; your assemblies are a stench to me. ²²Even though you bring me burnt offerings and grain offerings, I will not accept them. Though you bring choice fellowship offerings, I will have no regard for them. ²³Away with the noise of your songs! I will not listen to the music of your harps. ²⁴But let justice roll on like a river, righteousness like a never-failing stream! ²⁵"Did you bring me sacrifices and offerings forty years in the wilderness, people of Israel? ²⁶You have lifted up the shrine of your king, the pedestal of your idols, the star of your god—which you made for yourselves. ²⁷Therefore I will send you into exile beyond Damascus," says the* Lord, *whose name is God Almighty.*

Key Observation. God takes pleasure in our commitment to worship only when it matches our commitment to justice and righteousness.

Understanding the Word. Israel's confidence about the future likely proceeded from their worship. From the outside, their rituals appear proper and even exemplary. Every year, they travel to Bethel or Gilgal to celebrate the feasts of Passover/Unleavened Bread, Weeks/Pentecost, and Tabernacles/Booths (Exodus 12; Leviticus 23; Numbers 28–29; Deuteronomy 16). They keep the Sabbath and observe other holidays (e.g., Isaiah 1:13). They offer the prescribed sacrifices: the burnt offering (Leviticus 1:1–17; 6:8–13), the grain offering (2:1–16; 6:14–23), and the fellowship offerings (3:1–17; 7:11–36). And, of course, they play instruments and sing songs to the Lord. They've mastered their public displays of affection.

But God hates it. This is all for them, not him. Notice the repetition of "your" or "you" and "I." I reject *your* festivals. *I* can't stand the smell of *your* gatherings. *I* take no pleasure in *your* offerings. *I* cannot accept what *you're* bringing to the table. *I* can no longer listen to *your* songs and harps. The Lord names and refuses seven specific practices. In Hebrew, seven often symbolizes totality. So, God denounces *all* their worship.

At this point, the reason should no longer surprise us. God will not receive their expressions of love for him when they refuse to love others. He abhors the disparity. The incongruence empties devotion of any sincerity. The Lord wants their commitment to worship to match their commitment to justice and righteousness. If these don't flow like a consistent river or like a riverbed that's always in season, their worship services are simply for show.

After all, Israel didn't always worship this way. Even after God taught them how to approach him with sacrifices in Leviticus, there's no record of them regularly doing so in the wilderness. Amos, Jeremiah (2:2), and Hosea (2:14–15) all idealized Israel's faithfulness throughout those forty years. Numbers and Deuteronomy paint a different picture of that time. The people grumbled (Numbers 11), complained (Numbers 14), rebelled (Numbers 16), and resisted the Lord (Deuteronomy 1:26–28). But in comparison, the desert days now look good.

Verse 26 may be the hardest to understand in Amos. Therefore, translations can differ greatly. Some treat it as statement about Israel's current practices, "You have lifted [this] up" (e.g., NIV). Others read it as a proclamation about what Israel will do in exile, "You shall take [this] up" (e.g., NRSV and ESV). Some accuse Israel of lifting up a "shrine of your king" and a "pedestal of your idols" (e.g., NIV). Others indict Israel for taking up the specific Assyrian gods associated with Saturn—"Sakkuth/Sikkuth" and "Kaiwan/Kiyyun" (e.g., NRSV and ESV). However we read it, the verse connects Israel to idolatry.

Jesus said something similar about public worship in Matthew. Speaking about "that day" (probably the day of the Lord), he said that many will take pride in their religious activities or spiritual accomplishments. However, they will not enter God's kingdom because Jesus knows and welcomes those who *do* God's will (7:21–23). Yet—like Israel—many of us prioritize worship gatherings and minimize obedience. Whenever the church opens its doors, we're inside. But when we're outside, our doors, mouths, wallets, and schedules— indeed our very selves—are closed to the poor, orphan, widow, stranger, refugee, and even the family next door.

1. How much of yourself do you to give to organized religious activities and how much to ensuring justice for others?

2. If there's a significant imbalance, why?

T H R E E

The First Shall Be . . .

Amos 6:1–7 *Woe to you who are complacent in Zion, and to you who feel secure on Mount Samaria, you notable men of the foremost nation, to whom the people of Israel come! ²Go to Kalneha and look at it; go from there to great Hamath, and then go down to Gath in Philistia. Are they better off than your two kingdoms? Is their land larger than yours? ³You put off the day of disaster and bring near a reign of terror. ⁴You lie on beds adorned with ivory and lounge on your couches. You dine on choice lambs and fattened calves. ⁵You strum away on your harps like David and improvise on musical instruments. ⁶You drink wine by the bowlful and use the finest lotions, but you do not grieve over the ruin of Joseph. ⁷Therefore you will be among the first to go into exile; your feasting and lounging will end.*

Key Observation. God opposes the pursuit of pleasure when our pleasure is placed above everyone and everything else.

Understanding the Word. Amos's second woe surprisingly confronts both the Northern *and* the Southern Kingdom. Israel remains the prophet's primary target, but Judah lands within his crosshairs for the first time since Amos 2:4–5. He fires a warning shot to wake them from their self-confident stupor lest what will happen to Israel also happens to them. But then he quickly circles back to Samaria.

A few chapters ago, Amos chided Israel's wealthy women for their overindulgence (4:1–3). Now he admonishes her overconfident males—the leaders of the foremost (literally "first") nation. Israel's reported prominence may point to their privileged relationship with God, or more likely, to their pride. We can hear their arrogance when Amos quotes their nobles, who were saying something like "Look around! There's no one like us!" (6:2). Their pomposity fuels their sense of security.

On Day One of this week, we saw how Israel's inflated ego produced a longing for the day of the Lord. But now that Amos has revealed that day will actually be disastrous for Israel, they push the day away and they bring violence near. They ignore his warnings, carry on with their pretense, and perpetuate more injustice. Their arrogance manifests itself in luxurious living, fine dining, continuous merriment, and drunken depravity.

Israel's leading men live like royals. They sleep soundly on the same material as Solomon's throne (1 Kings 10:18; 2 Chronicles 9:17). They stretch out comfortably on couches like kings (e.g., 2 Samuel 4:7; 2 Samuel 11:2; Esther 1:6). They feast on the land's best meats just as Saul did (1 Samuel 28:21–24). They entertain themselves with David's instruments. They guzzled wine out of the holy bowls (e.g., Exodus 27:3; Numbers 7:13–85; 1 Kings 7:40–45). They anoint themselves with the best oil just as the prophets anointed Israel's kings (e.g., 1 Samuel 10:1).

But God declares their "feasting and lounging will end" (Amos 6:7). The word for "feasting" only occurs here and in Jeremiah 16:5. Jeremiah associates it with mourning. Amos's use implies that their carefree supper is actually a funeral reception. Israel's leaders unknowingly celebrate their own death.

Amos indicts those who are lying down, lounging around, eating well, strumming harps, writing songs, drinking wine, and smearing oil on themselves. Despite all of their frivolity, they're not getting sick (translated "grieve"). More specifically, they're not sickened by what they should be—the collapse of their kingdom. Therefore, Israel's "first" will be the first to go. Those who've led Israel into conceit, apathy, and excess will lead her into exile.

You may be asking what's so wrong with sleeping in, reclining by a pool, amusing ourselves with a novel, a show, or a song, indulging ourselves with some chocolate and a little wine, and lathering ourselves with essential oils? It sounds kind of nice, doesn't it? In and of themselves these things may not be bad. The Lord doesn't dislike pleasure; he created it. However, he does disapprove when we pursue personal pleasure over our relationship with him and at the expense of others. Luxury cannot take precedence over justice and righteousness. After all, "What good will it be for someone to gain the whole world, yet forfeit their soul?" (Matt. 16:26).

1. What value does our culture place on pleasure? What value do you place on it? Why?

2. What warnings do Amos's words have for us today?

FOUR

Silence

Amos 6:8–10 *The Sovereign* LORD *has sworn by himself—the* LORD *God Almighty declares:*

"I abhor the pride of Jacob and detest his fortresses; I will deliver up the city and everything in it."

⁹If ten people are left in one house, they too will die. ¹⁰And if the relative who comes to carry the bodies out of the house to burn them asks anyone who might be hiding there, "Is anyone else with you?" and he says, "No," then he will go on to say, "Hush! We must not mention the name of the LORD*."*

Key Observation. The Scriptures frequently summon us to be silent before God.

Understanding the Word. The Lord does not mince words. He abhors Israel's pride and detests his fortresses—the places that physically display the Northern Kingdom's hubris. On account of their arrogance, the Lord vows to take action against Israel. He previously swore to act by his holiness (Amos 4:2). This time he offers his own life as a pledge. These qualifiers intensify God's oaths. He will do what he says, and he will do so as the God of hosts—as the commander of heavenly armies (3:13; 4:13; 5:14–16, 27). (The NIV obscures the military connection by translating "the God of hosts" as "God Almighty.")

Amos illustrates their demise with a story that picks up where Amos 5:3 left off. A city sent one hundred men into battle, but only ten—only the smallest battalion—survived. For a while, they hid away in a home, but now they too will die. When their relative (possibly Judah) looks for a remnant among the rubble, they won't find anyone. Everyone will perish.

Strangely, their family comes to burn the bodies of the deceased. This is odd because Israel practiced a form of burial, not cremation. An Israelite's ideal burial ended with his/her bones being placed with the bones of his/her ancestors in the family's internment cave (e.g., Genesis 25:8, 17; 35:29; 49:29, 33). Burned bones can't be gathered. Therefore, most of the biblical references to body burning are negative (see Amos 2:1). In fact, the Old Testament typically connects cremation with criminal punishment (e.g., Genesis 38:24;

Leviticus 20:14; 21:9). This is what Amos has in mind. He depicts Israel's demise in the most reprehensible terms. They will die as criminals.

As the relative searches for survivors, someone tells him to be quiet and not to mention God's personal name—Yahweh. "Hush" is an uncommon command; it's used only seven times in the entire Old Testament. The prophets use it more often than anyone else. They require silence in the Lord's presence (Habakuk 2:20; Zechariah 2:13). Amos (6:10; 8:3) and Zephaniah (1:7) also demand it on the day of the Lord. When the Lord returns to Israel, he will come for judgment, not a conversation.

Judgment day isn't the only time the Bible summons us to silence. The author of Ecclesiastes encourages it whenever we approach God. "Guard your steps when you go to the house of God. Go near to listen rather than to offer the sacrifice of fools. . . . Do not be quick with your mouth, do not be hasty in your heart to utter anything before God. God is in heaven and you are on earth so let your words be few" (5:1–2). James recommends that we be "quick to listen" and "slow to speak," especially before the word of God (1:19).

Yet we fill our personal prayers and our corporate services with words. Why is that? If we're honest, silence disquiets us, so we quell it with noise. We keep talking, keep singing, and keep moving to avoid feeling uncomfortable. But when we do this, we often miss the Lord, who sometimes speaks to us in a "gentle whisper" (1 Kings 19:12).

1. How does silence make you feel? Why?

2. What is the relationship between silence and prayer?

FIVE

Rejoicing in Nothing

Amos 6:11–14 *For the Lord has given the command, and he will smash the great house into pieces and the small house into bits.*

¹²Do horses run on the rocky crags? Does one plow the sea with oxen? But you have turned justice into poison and the fruit of righteousness into bitterness— ¹³you who rejoice in the conquest of Lo Debar and say, "Did we not take Karnaim by our own strength?"

¹⁴For the Lᴏʀᴅ God Almighty declares, "I will stir up a nation against you, Israel, that will oppress you all the way from Lebo Hamath to the valley of the Arabah."

Key Observation. God's people pride themselves on what they've received from him, not what they've achieved for him.

Understanding the Word. We live most of our lives in our homes. They are our most important and intimate places. We eat, sleep, and relax at home. We tend to our marriages, raise our kids, and host our friends within their walls. When we're sick, tired, or sad we seek shelter under their roofs. We feel safe and known at home.

As this woe nears its end, the Lord strikes Israel where she feels the most secure. He shatters their homes. From the biggest (i.e., the king's) to the smallest, God commands his armies to demolish them all. He previously promised to smash the summer and winter homes of Israel's wealthiest citizens (Amos 3:15). Now no home is safe.

Amos characteristically drops in a couple of rhetorical questions to explain why. Of course, horses don't run on rocks. They would suffer serious injury if they tried. Of course, oxen can't plow the sea. They would drown if they did. These pictures are as preposterous as changing justice into poison or making the fruit of righteousness taste bitter (see Amos 5:7). This is what's happening in Israel. When the oppressed petition for aid, the courts administer toxins. When the righteous anticipate a sweet reward, others sour their expectations.

While this goes on, Israel celebrates its accomplishments. On the first day, we mentioned that Israel's economy boomed when they regained land along trade routes. This included Lo Debar and Karnaim. Lo Debar was likely a city on a highway in the Jordan River Valley. Karnaim was probably on the same highway but further north and east along the Yarmuk River. In verse 13, Amos quotes their boast, but he also undermines it. In the original language, Amos intentionally misspells Lo-Debar as Lo-Dabar, which means "nothing." According to Amos, Israel rejoices for nothing.

The final line returns to the theme of foreign invasion. Just as Egypt had done in the past (Exodus 3:9), a nation will oppress them in the future. They will subjugate Israel from Lebo Hamath to the Arabah. In Week One, we read about Jeroboam II's accomplishments. "He was the one who restored the boundaries of Israel from Lebo Hamath to the Dead Sea" (2 Kings 14:25). Other writers referred to the Dead Sea and its region as the Arabah (e.g., Deuteronomy 3:17). So, the invading army will overtake the *entire* nation and nullify *all* of the king's gains.

Throughout this woe, Amos meticulously undercuts everything Israel prides itself in—their international prominence, luxurious lifestyles, national defenses, comfortable homes, and military gains. Do these sound familiar? How often do we boast in our nation, pride ourselves in our possessions, flaunt our security, show off our houses, or brag about our accomplishments?

Like Israel, we often pride ourselves in the wrong things. We publicize our accomplishments and advertise our strengths. But Paul teaches us to boast in the Lord (e.g., 1 Corinthians 1:31) and in our weaknesses (e.g., 2 Corinthians 11:30). This seems odd and even awkward. So why would he say this? Because it's in our weaknesses, our struggles, our lack, and all that we are not that we realize all that Jesus is in us, for us, and through us (2 Corinthians 12:9–10).

1. What do you pride yourself in? Do you see these things as your accomplishments or evidence of God's grace?

2. What are the weak places in your life where God's strength is highlighted?

WEEK FIVE

GATHERING DISCUSSION OUTLINE

A. Open session in prayer.

B. View this week's video.

C. What general impressions and thoughts do you have after watching the video and reading the daily writings on these Scriptures? What, specifically, did this week's passages teach you about faith, life, and prayer?

D. Discuss selected questions from the daily readings. Always invite class members to share key insights or to raise questions that they found to be the most meaningful.

1. **KEY OBSERVATION**: Our confidence in the Lord's return should provoke us to faithful love.

DISCUSSION QUESTION: Who inspires you to faithful love? How?

2. **KEY OBSERVATION:** God takes pleasure in our commitment to worship only when it matches our commitment to justice and righteousness.

DISCUSSION QUESTION: How much of yourself do you to give to organized religious activities and how much to ensuring justice for others?

3. **KEY OBSERVATION:** God opposes the pursuit of pleasure when our pleasure is placed above everyone and everything else.

DISCUSSION QUESTION: What value does our culture place on pleasure? What value do you place on it? Why?

4. **KEY OBSERVATION:** The Scriptures frequently summon us to be silent before God.

    DISCUSSION QUESTION: What is the relationship between silence and prayer?

5. **KEY OBSERVATION:** God's people pride themselves on what they've received from him, not what they've achieved for him.

    DISCUSSION QUESTION: What are the weak places in your life where God's strength is highlighted?

E. Close session with prayer.

Amos 7

The Visions of Amos

ONE

Forming Locusts

Amos 7:1–3 ESV *This is what the Lord God showed me: behold, he was forming locusts when the latter growth was just beginning to sprout, and behold, it was the latter growth after the king's mowings.* *²When they had finished eating the grass of the land, I said,*

"O Lord God, please forgive! How can Jacob stand? He is so small!" ³The Lord relented concerning this: "It shall not be," said the Lord.

Key Observation. God attentively listens and faithfully responds to our prayers.

Understanding the Word. Chapter 7 launches us into the fifth major section in the book of Amos (7:1–8:3). This division features four visions that the Lord showed Amos. Biblical prophets frequently report receiving supernatural visions. These private experiences often propel them into public ministry (e.g., Isaiah 6; Jeremiah 1; Ezekiel 1–3). Accordingly, the Lord possibly reveals these things to Amos before he leaves Judah to prophesy in Israel.

God initially shows Amos that he is forming a swarm of locusts just as the second round of crops begin to produce vegetation. These brown grasshoppers pose a serious agricultural threat (e.g., Exodus 10; Amos 4:9). If they were to attack Israel at this time, they would devour the budding food supply and devastate the nation, particularly the peasant farmers. It appears that Israel's king already claimed the earlier harvest (i.e., the king's mowings in verse 1).

Consequently, everyone else would have to rely on the latter growth to sustain them through the summer. Without these resources, people would starve. The farming prophet knows this, so he intercedes on Israel's behalf.

Amos asks God to forgive Israel. He calls them "Jacob" to remind the Lord that he chose Esau's little brother, and to suggest they are weaker and more vulnerable than their boasts suggest (Amos 6). They couldn't survive an all-out agricultural catastrophe. When God hears Amos's prayer, he agrees not to unleash the locusts.

This isn't the only time the Lord changes his mind in response to prayer. In Exodus 32, while Moses met with God on Mount Sinai, Aaron fashioned a golden calf for the Israelites to worship. Their rebellion infuriated the Lord. He resolved to destroy them, so that he could build a new nation from Moses alone. But Moses urged God to spare his people. God listened and relented. Likewise, in the book of Judges, the Lord removed Israel's affliction when he hears their groaning (2:18). Then in Jonah, when the Ninevites repented, God dropped his disaster plan (3:10). This deeply angered Jonah, even though he already knew that God was "a gracious God and merciful, slow to anger and abounding in steadfast love, and relenting from disaster" (Jonah 4:2 ESV).

Thus, Amos appeals to God's compassion, and the Lord relents. But Amos didn't ask for this. He asked God to forgive Israel. Where's the disconnect? In Hebrew, God literally repents. He changes direction and withdraws his judgment. But, as we'll see, he does so only temporarily. Why? Because Israel doesn't repent. They refuse to change. For this reason, the Lord extends his patience—not his pardon. Yet God hears Amos's plea and it moves him. This is extraordinary!

The New Testament writers pick up on the power of prayer, especially James. In chapter 5, he tells those who are suffering to pray. He instructs those who are sick to ask the elders to intercede for them. When the Lord hears their prayer, he'll lift up that person. James encourages those who have sinned to confess and ask for prayer, so that the Lord may heal them. Because "the prayer of a righteous person has great power as it is working" (James 5:16 ESV). Of course, as with Amos, the Lord's answer may not match our requests. Nevertheless, he listens and responds in his time according to his wisdom.

1. Do you believe that God listens and responds to *your* prayers? Why or why not?

2. What impact does this have on the way you pray?

T W O

Calling for Fire

Amos 7:4–6 ESV *This is what the Lord God showed me: behold, the Lord God was calling for a judgment by fire, and it devoured the great deep and was eating up the land. [5]Then I said,*

"O Lord God, please cease! How can Jacob stand? He is so small!" [6]The Lord relented concerning this: "This also shall not be," said the Lord God.

Key Observation. Our heavenly Father invites us pray for others with perseverance and simplicity.

Understanding the Word. Today's vision—the second in this section—structurally matches the first. But instead of forming an insect horde, the Lord calls for fiery judgment. Fire imagery recurs throughout Amos. In the oracles against the nations (1:3–2:16), God vows to send fires that will devour every one of Israel's neighbor's strongholds (1:4, 7, 10, 12, 14; 2:2, 5). Then in the third judgment speech (Amos 5:1–17), the Lord warns Israel to seek him or he'll set the Northern Kingdom ablaze. In this final occurrence of fire in the book, it consumes the great deep and the land.

In the beginning, darkness covered the deep and the Spirit of God hovered over the waters. Then the Lord spoke light into existence and separated the waters into the waters above and the waters below (Genesis 1:2–8). Later, God opened up the great deep below and the windows of heaven above in order to flood the earth (Genesis 7:11; 8:2). Other writers refer to "the deep that crouches beneath"—presumably beneath the land (Genesis 49:25 ESV; Deuteronomy 33:13 ESV). In Amos, the great deep probably refers to the various underground sources of water as a collective group. This fire would burn so hot that even the subterranean water supplies would evaporate.

The word translated "land" specifically means a portion. The Old Testament writers frequently associate it with the land allotted to Israel's tribes. Most often, they use it when talking about Israel's priestly clan—the Levites—who did *not* receive a *portion* or an inheritance (e.g., Numbers 18:20; Deuteronomy 10:9). In Amos, it likely indicates that this fire would consume everything that the Lord gave Israel.

Amos understands what this means for an agrarian society, so he intercedes on Israel's behalf. This time, however, he doesn't ask God to forgive Israel. Perhaps he realizes this wasn't for him to ask, or perhaps he decides to ask God only to do what he had already done. Either way, he simply begs the Lord to stop because of Jacob's weaknesses. Again, God takes pity on his people and answers Amos's prayer.

This repetition calls our attention to three important aspects of prayer—intercession, perseverance, and simplicity. When he received the second vision, he prayed a second time for Israel. When he prayed, he offered a simple plea. "O Lord God, please forgive!" (7:2 esv); "O Lord God, please cease!" (7:5 esv).

In Luke 18:1–8, Jesus tells a story about a widow who continually petitioned a godless and compassionless judge to grant her justice. He repeatedly refused her request, but she kept pestering him. Eventually, he gave in. If an unrighteous judge will eventually respond to a widow's supplications, will not God answer his people's persistent cries? On this basis, Paul encourages us to "continue steadfastly in prayer" (Col. 4:2 esv).

In Matthew 6:7–13, Jesus instructs his disciples not to pray like people who ramble on and on because they think this will get God's attention. Alternatively, he tells us that our Father already knows what we need. Therefore, our prayers can be simple, childlike requests. For "how much more will your Father who is in heaven give good things to those who ask him!" (Matt. 7:11 esv).

1. Who in your life needs to experience the mercy of God? What would it look like for you to continually intercede for them?

2. Are you making prayer more complicated than it needs to be? If so, how can you simplify your prayers?

THREE
Not Measuring Up

Amos 7:7–9 ESV *This is what he showed me: behold, the Lord was standing beside a wall built with a plumb line, with a plumb line in his hand. ⁸And the* LORD *said to me, "Amos, what do you see?" And I said, "A plumb line." Then the Lord said,*

"Behold, I am setting a plumb line in the midst of my people Israel; I will never again pass by them; ⁹the high places of Isaac shall be made desolate, and the sanctuaries of Israel shall be laid waste, and I will rise against the house of Jeroboam with the sword."

Key Observation. God wants us to put our trust in him, instead of our strengths, social networks, or resources.

Understanding the Word. The central component of Amos's third vision is a plumb line . . . maybe. This word is unique to Amos. Most scholars agree that it indicates some kind of metal, perhaps tin or lead. Since the Lord holds this metal object in his hand while he stands next to a wall, a plumb line seems like a reasonable translation. Furthermore, other prophets employ a similar image (albeit using a different Hebrew word) in their pronouncements of judgment (e.g., 2 Kings 21:13; Isaiah 28:17).

What exactly is a plumb line? It typically consists of a metal weight tied to the end of string. Builders hold this tool against a wall to determine whether or not it is straight. Here the Lord uses it to see if Israel measures up to his standards. Clearly, they don't. But before Amos can intercede, God speaks. He asks Amos a question and then explains what will happen to the Northern Kingdom. The Lord will not pass them by for a third time, and Amos can see why. He knows Israel's time is up.

The vision's last verse targets three familiar institutions—the high places of Isaac, the sanctuaries of Israel, and the house of Jeroboam. None of Israel's establishments meet God's requirements for them. We discussed high places on Week One, Day Five. The Lord despises these local religious sites where people typically worship idols. Interestingly, Amos attributes the high places to Isaac. This may imply that he has Beer-sheba mind. The Northern Kingdom made pilgrimages to this city where God appeared to Isaac (Amos 5:5; Genesis 26:23–33). Wherever they are, the Lord will empty them. He will also ruin Israel's sanctuaries in Dan and Bethel, where Jeroboam I installed his golden calves (1 Kings 12:28–29). Finally, he will come against its monarchy with a sword.

We've said a lot about God's expectations for his sanctuaries and his courts. What does he expect of his kings? Deuteronomy 17 provides a pretty detailed list. In verses 14–20, God prohibits Israel's monarch from accumulating horses, wives, and riches. Instead, he must daily read God's laws, so that he can learn to fear God, obey the Lord's decrees, and not exalt himself and his interests above his fellow Israelites. Why does the Lord single out horses, wives, and riches? What do they represent?

In the ancient world, kings acquired horses to strengthen their military. They took additional wives, typically the daughters of foreign rulers, to solidify their international partnerships. They stored up riches to increase their economic power. Kings relied on their military capabilities, their political alliances, and their financial resources. But God asks this king to trust him instead.

Of course, these aren't just things that ancient kings trust. We count on their modern equivalents. We depend on our physical abilities, social networks, and financial investments to provide us with present peace and future security. We rely on them to accomplish our goals and advance our lives and careers. But these things are fleeting and ineffective. They ultimately can't deliver what we need. Only God can. Therefore, Jesus teaches us to seek God's kingdom and trust that God will give us everything we need (Matthew 6:25–34).

1. Where are you tempted to place your trust? How does that impact your life and your relationships with God and others?

2. What area of your life is hardest for you to entrust to God? How would your personal trust in God measure up to his plumb line?

FOUR

A Prophet, a Priest, and a King

Amos 7:10–13 ESV *Then Amaziah the priest of Bethel sent to Jeroboam king of Israel, saying, "Amos has conspired against you in the midst of the house of Israel. The land is not able to bear all his words. ¹¹For thus Amos has said,*

"'Jeroboam shall die by the sword, and Israel must go into exile away from his land.'"

¹²And Amaziah said to Amos, "O seer, go, flee away to the land of Judah, and eat bread there, and prophesy there, ¹³but never again prophesy at Bethel, for it is the king's sanctuary, and it is a temple of the kingdom."

Key Observation. When we're afraid, we often try to own what ultimately belongs to our God.

Understanding the Word. Yesterday's passage ends with a divine threat. The Lord will tear down the sanctuaries that Jeroboam I built in Dan and Bethel, and he will lift up his sword against the house of Jeroboam II in Samaria. The Northern Kingdom's religious and royal houses will share the same fate—total destruction. (In Hebrew, Amos's choice of vocabulary heightens this connection. "Shall be laid waste" and "sword" share three letters and sound similar.)

With this speech, Amos now constitutes a clear and present danger to the king and his kingdom. So Bethel's priest sends Jeroboam a warning. In it, Amaziah charges Amos with inciting a coup, and he expresses concern about the land's ability to contain the prophet's words. He is afraid that Amos's words are going to get out and cause trouble. The priest specifically reports the threats of assassination and exile. Most notably, Amaziah assigns all of these words to Amos—not to the Lord. Interestingly, Amos doesn't mention exile in the preceding three visions (7:1–8); he does in the following one (7:17).

The book of Amos doesn't record Jeroboam's response. However, we can assume it would align with Amaziah's words to Amos in verses 12–13. Amaziah starts off calling Amos a "seer." This may be an older designation for a prophet (1 Samuel 9:9), it may point to Amos's visions, or it may have become a derogatory term in the Northern Kingdom. The priest then orders Amos to run back to Judah. He wants him to go and earn his living as prophet there—not here in Bethel. For, according to Amaziah, Bethel is the "king's sanctuary" and "a temple of the kingdom."

These unusual descriptions reveal just how thoroughly Israel's temples depend on their king. They always have. When Jeroboam I established these temples, he installed his own priests in direct opposition to the divinely ordained Levitical priesthood (e.g., Numbers 1:49–54; 3:5–13; 1 Kings 12:31). In effect, he made priests, like Amaziah, political appointees. Then Jeroboam changed the date of one of Israel's three pilgrimage feasts—the Feast of Tabernacles or Booths—from the seventh month to the eighth (Leviticus 23:33–44; Deuteronomy 16:13–15; 1 Kings 12:32–33). This change violated God's directives and disconnected the festival from its founding purpose—to remember God's provision during the desert wanderings. He essentially created a new feast tied to his kingship. Finally, Jeroboam personally offered the new feast's sacrifices on the altar he made in Bethel (1 Kings 12:32–33). So much for checks and balances!

In Israel, the king controls everything. It's his priest, his sanctuary, and his temple. But his controls just mask his fears. They always have. Jeroboam I initiated his innovations because he was afraid that if Israel travelled to the Lord's temple in Jerusalem, their hearts would return to Judah's king. If that happened, they would kill him (1 Kings 12:27). Amos's words reveal that Amaziah and Jeroboam II share this fear and rely on similar tactics. They attempt to "protect" and "manage," and as a result, they co-opt what belongs to God for themselves. How often do we do the same?

1. What is your greatest fear? How do you try to control this fear? How does your attempt to control your fear hinder your ability to trust God?

2. What would it take for you to release your fears to God? Would you be willing to surrender your fear to God in prayer now?

FIVE

Not in This for the Money

Amos 7:14–17 ESV *Then Amos answered and said to Amaziah, "I was no prophet, nor a prophet's son, but I was a herdsman and a dresser of sycamore* *figs. ¹⁵But the* LORD *took me from following the flock, and the* LORD *said to me, 'Go, prophesy to my people Israel.' ¹⁶Now therefore hear the word of the* LORD.

"You say, 'Do not prophesy against Israel, and do not preach against the house of Isaac.'

¹⁷Therefore thus says the LORD:

"'Your wife shall be a prostitute in the city, and your sons and your daughters shall fall by the sword, and your land shall be divided up with a measuring line; you yourself shall die in an unclean land, and Israel shall surely go into exile away from its land.'"

Key Observation. God holds those with great influence to a greater standard.

Understanding the Word. After Amaziah opposes and seeks to banish Amos, God's prophet replies in kind. In doing so, Amos demonstrates how Amaziah actually opposes the Lord. Then he declares what will tragically happen to Amaziah, his family, and his country. In the end, Amaziah and his nation will be the ones who have to leave—not Amos. What Amaziah fears *will* come to pass.

Amos begins by correcting Amaziah's assumptions about his vocation. Amaziah presumes that Amos makes his living as a prophet. Subsequently, he encourages Amos to go and prophesy in Judah. Surely, he can earn enough money there to buy some bread (7:12). Amos, however, asserts that he's not in the prophetic business; he's an agriculturalist (7:14). Yet, like King David, the Lord took him from following the flock (2 Samuel 7:8; Psalm 78:70) and told him, "Go, prophesy to my people Israel" (7:15). Amos isn't prophesying for the money. This is not his occupation; it's his vocation—his divine calling. He doesn't speak for his own financial benefit; he speaks on God's behalf and under his direction. (Review Week One, Day Two for more on Amos as a prophet and farmer.)

Therefore, God's commands trump Amaziah's instructions. Though Amaziah says to go to Judah (7:12), God says to go to Israel (7:15). Though Amaziah says, "Do not prophesy against Israel, and do not preach against the house of Isaac" (7:16), the Lord says, "Prophesy to my people Israel" (7:15). For Amos, God determines the *where* and the *who*. By issuing Amos alternative orders, Amaziah challenges the Lord's authority. By silencing the prophets, he attempts to suppress God's word. By serving as Jeroboam's priest, Amaziah forsakes the Lord.

The consequences for Amaziah's actions directly relate to his priestly position. Amaziah will lose his wife, for a priest could not marry a prostitute (Leviticus 21:7). All of his children will die, and his priestly line will end. None of his offspring will take his place in Bethel's sanctuary. Foreigners will divide up his land and distribute it among themselves. They will take Amaziah and the rest of Israel to an unclean land—a land unfit for a priest. There he will die—defiled as well.

Judgment speeches like this one, though distressing to read, serve three important purposes. First, they confront offenders—those who violate God's decrees. Second, they comfort the oppressed—those hurt by others. Sin is inherently social; it always affects others. Finally, they caution others—people like you and me who study the Scriptures to learn how to live as God's people.

Amaziah's story particularly alerts leaders to the significance and seriousness of their roles. God calls priests to mediate between him and his people. He expects them to help his people draw near to his presence. Amaziah, however, abandons these divine responsibilities for personal and political gain. He intercedes between Jeroboam and Amos rather than God and his people. Consequently, the weight of the Lord's judgment will match the weight of Amaziah's post. With greater influence comes greater accountability. This is why James writes, "Not many of you should become teachers . . . for you know that we who teach will be judged with greater strictness" (James 3:1). Let's take this caution to heart and ask God to help us lead well.

1. Where or with whom has God given you influence?

2. What are you doing to insure that you don't abandon your responsibilities for personal gain?

WEEK SIX

GATHERING DISCUSSION OUTLINE

A. Open session in prayer.

B. View this week's video.

C. What general impressions and thoughts do you have after watching the video and reading the daily writings on these Scriptures? What, specifically, did this week's passages teach you about faith, life, and prayer?

D. Discuss selected questions from the daily readings. Always invite class members to share key insights or to raise questions that they found to be the most meaningful.

    1. **KEY OBSERVATION**: God attentively listens and faithfully responds to our prayers.

    DISCUSSION QUESTION: Do you believe that God listens and responds to *your* prayers? Why or why not?

    2. **KEY OBSERVATION:** Our heavenly Father invites us pray for others with perseverance and simplicity.

    DISCUSSION QUESTION: Who in your life needs to experience the mercy of God? What would it look like for you to continually intercede for them?

    3. **KEY OBSERVATION:** God wants us to put our trust in him, instead of our strengths, social networks, or resources.

DISCUSSION QUESTION: What area of your life is hardest for you to entrust to God? How would your personal trust in God measure up to his plumb line?

4. **KEY OBSERVATION:** When we're afraid, we often try to own what ultimately belongs to our God.

    DISCUSSION QUESTION: What is your greatest fear? How do you try to control this fear? How does your attempt to control your fear hinder your ability to trust God?

5. **KEY OBSERVATION:** God holds those with great influence to a greater standard.

    DISCUSSION QUESTION: Where or with whom has God given you influence?

E. Close session with prayer.

Amos 8

The Judgment of Israel

ONE

The End

Amos 8:1–3 NRSV *This is what the Lord G*OD *showed me—a basket of summer fruit.* ²*He said, "Amos, what do you see?" And I said, "A basket of summer fruit." Then the L*ORD *said to me,*

"The end has come upon my people Israel; I will never again pass them by. ³*The songs of the temple shall become wailings in that day," says the Lord G*OD*; "the dead bodies shall be many, cast out in every place. Be silent!"*

Key Observation. When we encounter challenging Scriptures, perhaps our first response should be a humble, reflective, and prayerful silence through which we draw near to God.

Understanding the Word. Though these verses begin a new week for us and a new chapter in Amos, they actually conclude the book's fifth major section. It starts with three visions. Amos sees the Lord forming locusts (7:1–3), calling for a fiery rain (7:4–6), and standing beside a wall with a plumb line in hand (7:7–9). Amos then spars with Amaziah (7:10–17) before he shares his fourth and final vision.

This one begins like all the others, but it develops like the third (7:7–9). God shows Amos something, he asks the prophet what he sees, and he explains what it means. Unlike the first two, Amos does not pray, and God does not relent. Instead, the picture portrays Israel's imminent end in graphic detail.

Amos sees a basket filled with summer fruit. There's nothing ominous about a fruit basket. Locusts devour crops, fire burns whatever it touches, and the plumb line exposes Israel's crookedness. But a basket of ready-to-eat figs and pomegranates just looks tasty. Right? Yes, but the crux of this passage is not found in what Amos sees but in what he hears. The Hebrew word for "fruit" sounds just like the word for "end." Despite Israel's bountiful appearance, her time has come. They've exhausted their chances to repent, and they are ripe for judgment. Therefore, God will never again pass by without reaping his people.

The vision climaxes with another depiction of the day of the Lord as the end of Israel—a day of judgment and death rather than salvation and life (Amos 5:18–20). On that day, the temple's songs will become laments. Israel's worshippers will wail rather than rejoice. Dead bodies will pile up everywhere; there will be too many to properly bury them all. In the end, there's only silence.

This rare demand for silence occurs for the second time in Amos. In Amos 6:10, a family member searches for survivors among the dead. When he finds no one, someone says, "Hush! We must not mention the name of the LORD" (see Week Five, Day Four). In both occurrences, the call for quiet occurs in the aftermath of judgment and in the presence of death. Perhaps this is only fitting.

Truthfully, most of us are not sure how to respond to Amos's descriptions of Israel's collapse or any of the other biblical accounts of human violence or divine vengeance. We frankly try to avoid them, but Amos doesn't afford us that option. So, what options *do* we have? We could reasonably excuse all of these texts as figures of speech. We could judge verses like these to be primitive and irrelevant to our time. We could reject these Scriptures and maybe even the God they reveal as immoral.

There are other options, of course. But perhaps our first response should be a particular kind of silence. A humble silence that acknowledges the limits of our knowledge and perspective. A reflective silence that seriously ponders what these passages teach us about God and ourselves. A prayerful silence that brings all of our questions and emotions to the God whose perfect perspective and incomparable character can be trusted.

1. Do you typically avoid, rationalize, judge, or reject difficult passages in the Bible? Why?

2. What would it look like for you to respond with humble silence instead?

TWO

Out of Balance

Amos 8:4–6 NRSV *Hear this, you that trample on the needy, and bring to ruin the poor of the land, ⁵saying, "When will the new moon be over so that we may sell grain; and the sabbath, so that we may offer wheat for sale? We will make the ephah small and the shekel great, and practice deceit with false balances, ⁶buying the poor for silver and the needy for a pair of sandals, and selling the sweepings of the wheat."*

Key Observation. God cares as much about how we make money as what we do with it.

Understanding the Word. Right after God shows Amos a vision of Israel's end, he reminds everyone why this is happening. Back in Amos 2:6–8, the Lord delivers his first indictment against the Northern Kingdom. Here he revisits the theme of economic injustice and illuminates the ends, motive, and means of Israel's exploitation of the poor.

He demands the perpetrators' attention. Then he addresses them according to their crime and its outcome. They take advantage of the needy, and they literally bring them to an end. To put it bluntly, they are killing the poor. Their business practices directly result in higher rates of hunger, indentured servitude, and death among the needy.

Israel's rich solely want to maximize their monetary gains, especially since the new moon and Sabbath limit their opportunities. At the beginning of each month (i.e., the new moon) and the end of each week (i.e., the Sabbath), the Lord invites his people to worship him. As part of their Sabbath celebrations and apparently their new moon festivals, God's people don't work (e.g., Exodus 20:8–11; Deuteronomy 5:12–15). But rather than rejoicing in the Lord's rest, the prosperous are annoyed at how worship cuts into their profits. They want the services to end so they can get back to business.

To make up for their losses, they violate God's laws and cheat others, particularly the impoverished (e.g., Leviticus 19:35–36; Proverbs 11:1; 16:11; Ezekiel 45:10–12). They reduce the volume of the ephah—the standard grain measurement—so that people receive less than they pay for. They increase the density of the shekel—the standard balance weight—so that people pay more than they should. They also use inaccurate balances to tip every transaction even further in their favor. On top of all this, they sweep out the bottom of the storage bin and call it "wheat." They sell a smaller than advertised amount of inferior product at an inflated rate. It's a highly effective, extremely unethical, and entirely too familiar business model.

When this happens, the rich become richer and the poor become cheap slaves. The Lord initially charges Israel with *selling* "the righteous for silver, and the needy for a pair of sandals" (2:6 NRSV). The powerful force the impoverished into slavery to cover minor debts. Now God accuses the wealthy of "*buying* the poor for silver and the needy for a pair of sandals" (8:6 NRSV; italics added). In this system, the affluent not only precipitate the problem; they benefit from it. The wealthy press others into debt slavery, and then they purchase these slaves at reduced prices.

Besides changing the verb, the Lord makes a more subtle and more significant amendment. He replaces "*the righteous*" with "*the poor*." The two are often synonymous in the Scriptures. For example, Matthew records Jesus blessing "the poor in spirit" (5:3), but in Luke's gospel Jesus simply blesses "you who are poor" (6:20). We tend to think that the righteous are rich. But the Bible reminds us that poverty can follow faithfulness, and vice versa, prosperity can stem from sin. Therefore, we should examine our business and financial practices. If we unjustly gain at other's expense, we must right the scales. If we lose for others and the Lord, we wait for a better reward.

1. Have you unjustly gained at someone else's expense? Did you make it right? If not, what can you do today?

2. Do you financially sacrifice for others and for God? How might you live more simply to give more generously?

THREE

Trembling and Turning

Amos 8:7–10 NRSV *The Lord has sworn by the pride of Jacob: Surely I will never forget any of their deeds. [8]Shall not the land tremble on this account, and* *everyone mourn who lives in it, and all of it rise like the Nile, and be tossed about and sink again, like the Nile of Egypt?*

⁹On that day, says the Lord GOD, I will make the sun go down at noon, and darken the earth in broad daylight. ¹⁰I will turn your feasts into mourning, and all your songs into lamentation; I will bring sackcloth on all loins, and baldness on every head; I will make it like the mourning for an only son, and the end of it like a bitter day.

Key Observation. We can grieve with hope because we know the God who raises the dead.

Understanding the Word. For the third time, the Lord takes an oath of action. He devotes himself to end Israel's commercial malpractice (8:4–6). Previously, he swears by his holiness (4:2) and by himself (6:8). This time he swears, curiously, by "the pride of Jacob." He condemns this in 6:8, so why does he pledge by it now? Some read this phrase as a title like the "Glory of Israel" (1 Sam. 15:29). Others maintain it refers to Israel's land (Psalm 47:4). More likely, the Lord applies it ironically and a bit sarcastically. His resolve is as unwavering as their arrogance.

With another rhetorical question, God stresses the inevitably of his judgment. As surely as the Nile River floods and then recedes, the land will shake on account of Israel's corruption. This trembling may allude to the earthquake mentioned in Amos 1:1. If so, it would explain why everyone mourns and what smashes their houses (6:11).

Verse 9 circles back to the day of the Lord and reinforces its cosmic effect. In Amos 5:18–20, he insists that day will be a day of darkness and not light for Israel. Here he depicts it as a solar eclipse. In the middle of the day, the sun will disappear, and the earth will turn dark. Scholars debate whether or not Amos predicts an actual eclipse. Unlike the earthquake, the book does not explicitly mention this event anywhere else. Nevertheless, it fits the book's general tenor and would certainly terrify Amos's audience.

Not only will the Lord change the day to night, he will turn Israel's celebrations into burials and their rejoicing into mourning (Amos 5:16). In turn, Israel will wear their grief. They will dress in sackcloth and shave their heads, which are the customary signs of sorrow (e.g., Genesis 37:34; Isaiah 22:12; Ezekiel 7:18). But there will not be anything customary about their tears. They will weep like a parent weeps at the death of her only child. They will mourn as people without hope—without a future. In the end, the day will only be bitter.

This passage contains the fifth and final occurrence of a key word in Amos. The basic meaning and most common translation of the word is "turn." It can also mean "turn over" or "transform." Amos attributes this action to both the Israelites and God. Israel "turns" justice to wormwood and poison—to something bitter and deadly (5:7; 6:12). The Lord "overthrows" cities (4:11), he "transforms" darkness and light (5:8), and he "turn[s]" festivals into funerals (8:10). Israel's turning requires the Lord's overturning. What they turned bitter for others, he will turn bitter for them.

Though there's no hope for Israel here, there is hope for us. Another prophet speaks of a time after Israel's demise and Judah's exile when God will turn his people's mourning back into joy (Jeremiah 31:13). As Christians, we believe God accomplished this through the death and resurrection of Jesus. Therefore, even though we grieve death, we don't do so as those who have no hope; for we know the God that turns death to life (1 Thessalonians 4:13).

1. What in your life are you grieving?

2. How is the resurrection of Jesus shaping your grief?

FOUR

A Famine like No Other

Amos 8:11–12 NRSV *The time is surely coming, says the Lord GOD, when I will send a famine on the land; not a famine of bread, or a thirst for water, but of hearing the words of the LORD. ¹²They shall wander from sea to sea, and from north to east; they shall run to and fro, seeking the word of the LORD, but they shall not find it.*

Key Observation. Our lives wholly depend on the word of God.

Understanding the Word. The Lord speaks more than fifty times in the book of Amos. In the vast majority, God addresses his people through his prophet, who uses some variation of the messenger formula—"Thus says the Lord." Then on five occasions, God commands Israel to hear his word

(3:1; 4:1; 5:1; 7:16; 8:4). However, Israel not only fails to listen; they put out a prophetic gag order to mute God (2:12; 7:12–13, 16). They will eventually get what they want.

In the coming days, the Lord will stop speaking to Israel. He will withdraw his prophets, and his people will hear nothing. Only then will they finally realize they can't live without God's word. It's as essential to their survival as bread and water. Therefore, they will frantically search for God's word as they once did for water (4:7–8). They will "wander" like they did in the desert (Numbers 32:13) or "tremble" like they did at Sinai (Exodus 20:18). They will desperately scour the land in every direction, but they won't find what they seek.

The absolute necessity of God's word and its association with bread traces back to Deuteronomy's retelling of Israel's wilderness years. Chapter 8 recounts how the Lord let Israel hunger, and then supernaturally fed them with manna—a sweet wafer-like substance that fell each day with the morning dew (Exodus 16:11–36; Numbers 11:4–9). Deuteronomy contends that the Lord provided for Israel in this way to humble them and to teach them, "one does not live by bread alone, but by every word that comes from the mouth of the LORD" (Deut. 8:3).

In Matthew 4:4, Jesus quotes Deuteronomy 8:3 when the Spirit leads him into the wilderness where he fasts for forty days and nights. Jesus is ravenously hungry when the devil tempts him to prove his divine status and power by turning rocks into bread. Jesus refuses. He knows that in order to live he needs God's word more than food. If this is true for Jesus, how much more is it true for us?

John's gospel expands this in a different direction. In his opening chapter, he boldly and beautifully illustrates that Jesus *is* the eternal Word of God (John 1:1–14). Then in chapter 6, Jesus proclaims that he *is* the bread of life (v. 35). He *is* the manna who "comes down from heaven and gives life to the world" (v. 33). Therefore, whoever comes to him (v. 35), eats his flesh and drinks his blood (vv. 52–55), and abides in him (v. 56) "will live forever" (v. 58). This so confounds Jesus' first followers that many of them leave him (v. 66). But when Jesus asks his core twelve disciples if they too want to leave, Simon Peter answers, "Lord, to whom can we go? You have the words of eternal life" (vv. 67–68). For John, Jesus both *is* and *has* the life-giving word of God.

These Scriptures imply that above all else we depend on God's word. For by his word, God creates and sustains all things (Genesis 1; Hebrews 1:3). His word guides (Psalm 119:105) and his word saves (James 1:21). All of our other cravings—every hunger and thirst—ultimately point to our true need.

1. In this season of your life, what is your deepest longing? Why is this particularly acute?

2. How might this desire point beyond itself and ultimately be filled by Jesus?

FIVE

Stop Swearing

Amos 8:13–14 NRSV *In that day the beautiful young women and the young men shall faint for thirst.* *[14]Those who swear by Ashimah of Samaria, and say, "As your god lives, O Dan," and, "As the way of Beer-sheba lives"—they shall fall, and never rise again.*

Key Observation. Our words matter to God and others, so truth-telling and promise-keeping should mark our lives.

Understanding the Word. Without God's word to quench their thirst (8:11), Israel's youthful men and women, those in the prime of life who represent Israel's future generations, will grow faint and weak. Their failure to find what they critically need parallels the inability of Israel's swift, strong, courageous, and military-trained to evade God's wrath (2:14–16). The young's inevitable collapse also recalls the Lord's eulogy, in which he envisions Israel as a fallen virgin (5:2). All of this reinforces the indispensability of God's word. The word Israel despises is the word they require.

God's primary grievance with Israel in this passage is by whom or what they swear. Like us, they call on things greater than themselves to back or vouch for them. Israel's vows unveil where her confidence lies. In Deuteronomy, the Lord required that his people make oaths only by his name (6:13). Here Israel obligates themselves by three other things.

First, they swear by Ashimah of Samaria. "Ashimah" may refer to an idol created by the people of Hamath (2 Kings 17:30)—a region that Jeroboam II regains for Israel (2 Kings 14:28). However, some scholars argue this is Asherah—a Canaanite goddess that Israel often worships (e.g., Judges 3:7). Others propose it simply means "shame" and suggest the "shame of Samaria" points to the golden calf in Bethel—Samaria's sanctuary (Amos 7:13). Second, they commit themselves by the god of Dan, which certainly points to Israel's other golden calf (1 Kings 12:28–30). Finally, they pledge by the way of Beer-sheba. This probably invokes Israel's pilgrimages (Amos 5:5). Various academics have proposed it refers to other gods in order to maintain symmetry between these oaths. However we read these phrases, they prove Israel's apostasy.

The choice of Samaria, Dan, and Beer-sheba likely symbolizes the totality of Israel's sin. Its capital city Samaria represents the nation's center of power and its king. As the northernmost city in Israel and the southernmost city in Judah, the joint mention of Dan and Beer-sheba signifies all of Canaan and its inhabitants (e.g., Judges 20:1; 1 Samuel 3:20). From its heart to its edges, all of Israel is complicit. Therefore, every last one of them will fall, and none of them will recover (Amos 5:2).

The Bible's instructions about swearing take an interesting turn with Jesus. Apparently in the first century, the people of God's primary problem is not swearing by other gods. It's swearing by things associated with God and then not fulfilling their promises. When this happens, their vows become lies and their assertions become manipulations. They become false and violate another Old Testament command—"do not swear falsely by my name" (Lev. 19:12). So, in Matthew 5, Jesus tells us to not swear at all; instead, our speech must be direct and honest (vv. 33–37).

Our world increasingly believes that words cannot be trusted. We live in an age of fake news, false advertising, political cover-ups, Ponzi schemes, corporate spin, and broken contracts. Perhaps more than ever, people need others they can trust. As God's people, let's be those people. Let's tell the truth and keep our promises.

1. Do others trust you? Why or why not?

2. Are you direct and honest or do you exaggerate and embellish?

WEEK SEVEN

GATHERING DISCUSSION OUTLINE

A. Open session in prayer.

B. View this week's video.

C. What general impressions and thoughts do you have after watching the video and reading the daily writings on these Scriptures? What, specifically, did this week's passages teach you about faith, life, and prayer?

D. Discuss selected questions from the daily readings. Always invite class members to share key insights or to raise questions that they found to be the most meaningful.

1. **KEY OBSERVATION**: When we encounter challenging Scriptures, perhaps our first response should be a humble, reflective, and prayerful silence through which we draw near to God.

   DISCUSSION QUESTION: Do you typically avoid, rationalize, judge, or reject difficult passages in the Bible? Why?

2. **KEY OBSERVATION:** God cares as much about how we make money as what we do with it.

   DISCUSSION QUESTION: Have you unjustly gained at someone else's expense? Did you make it right? If not, what can you do today?

3. **KEY OBSERVATION:** We can grieve with hope because we know the God who raises the dead.

DISCUSSION QUESTION: How is the resurrection of Jesus shaping your grief?

4. **KEY OBSERVATION:** Our lives wholly depend on the word of God.

   DISCUSSION QUESTION: In this season of your life, what is your deepest longing? Why is this particularly acute?

5. **KEY OBSERVATION:** Our words matter to God and others, so truth-telling and promise-keeping should mark our lives.

   DISCUSSION QUESTION: Are you direct and honest or do you exaggerate and embellish?

E. Close session with prayer.

Amos 9

The Shaking and Salvation of Israel

ONE

Nowhere to Go

Amos 9:1–4 *I saw the Lord standing by the altar, and he said:*

"Strike the tops of the pillars so that the thresholds shake. Bring them down on the heads of all the people; those who are left I will kill with the sword. Not one will get away, none will escape. ²Though they dig down to the depths below, from there my hand will take them. Though they climb up to the heavens above, from there I will bring them down. ³Though they hide themselves on the top of Carmel, there I will hunt them down and seize them. Though they hide from my eyes at the bottom of the sea, there I will command the serpent to bite them. ⁴Though they are driven into exile by their enemies, there I will command the sword to slay them.

"I will keep my eye on them for harm and not for good."

Key Observation. God's presence is limitless; it extends even to the places we least expect.

Understanding the Word. Congratulations! You've made it to final week in our study through the book of Amos. As you now thoroughly know, this is not an easy book. Amos's judgments are severe, its images are distressing, and its forecast is dim. The concluding chapter delivers more of the same until the last five verses.

Chapter 9 starts with another vision. This vision combines two of the recurring means of judgment in Amos—an earthquake and an invading army.

Amos sees the Lord standing beside "*the* altar," and commanding his armies to destroy the surrounding temple. This is probably Bethel's altar and sanctuary (Amos 3:14; 4:4; 5:5–6; 7:13). God instructs his heavenly hosts to strike the top of the temple's support columns with enough force to shake the posts right off their bases and shatter them upon the worshippers' heads. Those who survive or escape before the building collapses will encounter their enemy's sword.

Ultimately, no Israelite will elude God's judgment (2:13–16). No matter how low they dig, how high they climb, or how far they go, God will find them and judge them. It's not surprising that God can reach the heavens or the mountaintops; we normally associate him with things above. However, it is surprising that the Lord stretches to the depths below, literally to Sheol—the realm of the dead (e.g., 1 Samuel 2:6). It's shocking that the sea serpent obeys his commands. It's startling that even in exile Israel will not find shelter from his wrath. His judgment knows no bounds.

Wherever Israel goes, God will fix his eyes upon them, but his gaze will not bring blessing or salvation. The Lord will stare them down to destroy them. This is not what God's people expect, but it is what they seek. They search for evil, and they love it (Amos 5:14–15). Therefore, the Lord assures they will receive it. In fact, they cannot escape it.

While Amos emphasizes the inescapability of God's judgment, Psalm 139 stresses the universality of his presence, and Romans 8 accentuates the certainty of his love for those in Christ. The psalmist insists that if he ascends the heavens, sleeps with the dead, rises with the sun, or dwells beyond the sea, the Lord will be there (Psalm 139:7–10). Paul contends "neither death nor life, neither angels nor demons, neither the present nor the future, nor any powers, neither height nor depth, nor anything else in all creation, will be able to separate us from the love of God that is in Christ Jesus our Lord" (Rom. 8:38–39).

Amos's assertions about God's anger and Paul's proclamation in Romans about God's affection build upon the psalmist's foundation. Because God's presence knows no limits, he can enact justice and uphold his promises everywhere and for everybody. Neither you nor I, neither anyone nor anything in your life, my life, or anyone else's life falls outside the range of God's presence. At times, this realization should rattle us, and at times, it should reassure us. When, like Israel, we oppose God's will, we will experience his presence as disturbing judgment. When we do God's will as the Holy Spirit enables us, we will experience his presence as unfailing love.

1. Where in your life do you not expect God's presence? Why?

2. Where and how are you currently experiencing God's presence?

T W O

Incomparable Power

Amos 9:5–6 *The Lord, the* LORD *Almighty—he touches the earth and it melts, and all who live in it mourn; the whole land rises like the Nile, then sinks like the river of Egypt;* ⁶*he builds his lofty palace in the heavens and sets its foundation on the earth; he calls for the waters of the sea and pours them out over the face of the land—the* LORD *is his name.*

Key Observation. God displays his incomparable power through the perceived weakness of sacrificial love.

Understanding the Word. Yesterday's verses highlight God's pervasive presence. Today's passage focuses on his immeasurable power. God is present everywhere, *and* he is able to do whatever he wills. Israel believes his power will only aid them. They expect the Lord will always act *for* them and never *against* them. But once again, they presume wrongly.

Amos reminds Israel that the Lord of hosts could melt the world with a simple touch. He could cause the ground to rise and fall like a river (Amos 8:8). In other words, God can judge with fire or an earthquake (e.g., 1:1, 4). After all, he is the God who builds the heavens, establishes the earth, and commands the seas. Here he explicitly constructs either a stairway (e.g., Ezekiel 40) or an upper chamber (e.g., Psalm 104) in the heavens. He lays the foundation of something well-built on the earth. This may be a vault similar to the dome or expanse that separates the waters above from the waters below in Genesis 1:6. A vault fits with the references to the seas and the flood (Amos 5:8). For the Lord calls the seas (Genesis 1:10) and empties the waters to flood the earth (Genesis 6–8).

The song emphasizes that all of creation is God's design *and* his domain. He creates *and* controls all of it. Therefore, the Lord can exercise his power over every part of his world and over every person who inhabits it. He may exert his power to save *or* to condemn. Amos accentuates the later. If God can torch the earth and cause global mourning, then he can accomplish everything Amos prophecies.

Though Amos primarily affirms the Lord's power to destroy, he bookends these verses with God's personal name—Yahweh. His name always recalls the exodus and his power to deliver (e.g., Exodus 15:6). The Lord's victory over Egypt and his rescue of Israel epitomize his power in the Old Testament. He plagued Egypt with ten terrifying signs that culminated in the death of Egypt's firstborn sons (Exodus 7:14–12:32). But he spared his people, parted the sea, provided them with food and water, made a covenant with them, and filled their tabernacle with his glory (Exodus 12:1–24:18; 40:34–38). He demonstrated his power with profound strength.

Subsequently, God's people suppose the Lord will always act in a similar manner. This is why so many disregarded Jesus. Rather than wielding his divine power in similar ways, Jesus sacrificed himself on a cross (2 Corinthians 13:4). But God raised him from the dead and proved the incomparable power of love exercised in weakness (1 Corinthians 1:25). This seems ridiculous in a world that favors and promotes strength. But it's the power of the self-giving love of God that ultimately saves us from sin and death and transforms us here and now (e.g., 1 Corinthians 1:18; 2 Corinthians 12:9). Jesus invites us to follow him in the "weak" way of love. He then promises that when we expend our lives for God and other, we will find true life (Luke 9:23–27).

1. What does our culture view as powerful? Why?

2. In what tangible ways can you display the self-giving love of God to others this week?

THREE

Sift All, Save Some

Amos 9:7–10 *"Are not you Israelites the same to me as the Cushites?" declares the* LORD. *"Did I not bring Israel up from Egypt, the Philistines from Caphtor and the Arameans from Kir?*

⁸"Surely the eyes of the Sovereign LORD *are on the sinful kingdom. I will destroy it from the face of the earth. Yet I will not totally destroy the descendants of Jacob," declares the* LORD. *⁹"For I will give the command, and I will shake the people of Israel among all the nations as grain is shaken in a sieve, and not a pebble will reach the ground. ¹⁰All the sinners among my people will die by the sword, all those who say, 'Disaster will not overtake or meet us.'"*

Key Observation. God always and only saves us by his grace.

Understanding the Word. After announcing that his presence and power will confront rather than comfort Israel, the Lord poses two rhetorical questions. These questions directly undermine the objections Israel will likely raise on the basis of their relationship and history with God. First, the Lord declares that he regards Israel no differently than the comparatively irrelevant Cushites (i.e., Ethiopians or Nubians). Then more shockingly God announces that as he brought Israel out of Egypt, he also took Israel's arch rivals—the Philistines and the Arameans—from their homelands and made them the Northern Kingdom's neighbors. In other words, Israel is not as special as they think. Therefore, they shouldn't expect immunity from the judgment on account of their election or the exodus.

Instead, the Lord's gaze remains fixed on the "sinful kingdom," and he will destroy it (Amos 9:8). However, at the end of verse 8, God backs off his threat to completely annihilate "the descendants of Jacob" (literally "the house of Jacob"). This contradicts or at least mitigates what the Lord previously pledged, with the possible exception of Amos 5:14–16. The key to understanding the change lies in the distinction between "the sinful kingdom" and "the house of Jacob," and the subsequent mention of "sinners" (9:10). Israel's political structures and leaders—its king, sanctuaries, and courts—and the elite who perpetuate the kingdom's sin will die by the sword. However, the Lord will spare those in Jacob's house who remain faithful to him.

Lest Israel become too comfortable or hopeful, God quickly returns to his pronouncement of judgment. He will still shake and sift Israel alongside every other nation. Israelite farmers used a large metal sieve to separate grain from anything else they gathered with it. The grain would pass through while the debris would be caught and discarded. Likewise, the Lord will remove the sinners contaminating God's people and falsely claiming divine protection.

While Israel's "pebbles" will die by the sword, the filter image subtly reinforces the salvation of a few kernels. In this way, the Lord will fulfill his promise not to completely destroy his people (e.g., Leviticus 26:44; Deuteronomy 4:31, etc.). Amos's contemporaries in the Southern Kingdom of Judah spoke even more strongly about the Lord securing a remnant. Isaiah foretold of a time when God would recover Israel's exiles from around the world (Isaiah 11:11–12). Similarly, Micah prophesied that the Lord will gather Israel's survivors (Micah 2:12).

Paul appeals to the prophetic promise to save some of Israel in Romans. In chapters 9–11, he addresses several questions about God's faithfulness to Israel in light of Jesus and the inclusion of Gentiles (non-Jews) in God's people. For Paul, the Jews who have accepted Jesus prove that God has not rejected Israel; instead, he has preserved a remnant by his grace (11:5–6). In fact, whenever and whoever God saves, he always and only saves us by grace. Salvation is a gift that we receive by faith and with faithfulness. Most of Israel forgot the second half. They abandoned their faith and lived faithlessly. Hoping that we don't follow their ways, the New Testament writers urge us to live lives worthy of God's gift by "bearing fruit in every good work, growing in the knowledge of God" (Col. 1:10).

1. How have you recently grown in your knowledge of God's grace?

2. What pebbles and branches does the Lord want to sift out of your life?

FOUR

Restoration and Expansion

Amos 9:11–12 *"In that day*

"I will restore David's fallen shelter—I will repair its broken walls and restore its ruins—and will rebuild it as it used to be, ¹²so that they may possess the remnant of Edom and all the nations that bear my name," declares the LORD, who will do these things.

Acts 15:15–18 *The words of the prophets are in agreement with this, as it is written:*

¹⁶"'After this I will return and rebuild David's fallen tent. Its ruins I will rebuild, and I will restore it, ¹⁷that the rest of mankind may seek the Lord, even

all the Gentiles who bear my name, says the Lord, who does these things' [18]things known from long ago."

Key Observation. In and through Jesus, God does what Amos prophesies—he incorporates the nations into his family.

Understanding the Word. The final verses of Amos are by far the most hopeful. They cast Israel's attention to a day of restoration in the distant future. Everywhere else in Amos, the day of the Lord points to Israel's impending judgment (e.g., Amos 2:16; 3:14, etc.). These verses look beyond the day of destruction to a subsequent day of salvation. In particular, they signal a return from exile and a reestablishment of Israel's life in the land.

At that time, the Lord will lift up David's fallen shelter. The mention of David is a bit perplexing, and the meaning of the word "shelter" is unclear. Some scholars interpret David's hut as a reference to Jerusalem or the Southern Kingdom of Judah. However, Judah and its capital won't fall for about 150 years, and their restoration would give Israel little consolation. Others believe the word refers to the city Sukkoth. The Psalms associate this place with David's military victories (Psalms 60:6–12; 108:7–13), so here it could symbolize a return to power. More likely, the booth (ESV) indicates the United Kingdom under David. The phrase "as it used to be" may support this claim. Micah uses the same phrase when he prophesies that a new king will come from David's hometown Bethlehem and rule over Israel (Micah 5:2).

The Lord positions the reunification and the reconstruction of David's kingdom within his global purposes. The Lord will restore Israel so that they may incorporate Edom and the nations upon whom God's name was called. God may single out Edom because they descend from Jacob's older brother Esau (Genesis 36:1). Despite the brothers' reconciliation (Genesis 33), their offspring are enemies (e.g., Numbers 20:14–21; 2 Kings 8:20, etc.). Edom's inclusion would constitute a family reconciliation. The admittance of "all the nations that bear my name" may literally be every nation or more modestly the nations named in Amos.

At a pivotal moment in the book of Acts, James, Jesus' brother, quotes this passage and interprets "all nations" inclusively. The leaders of the church were meeting in Jerusalem to debate whether or not Gentile Christians must be circumcised and keep the law of Moses (15:6). After listening to various testimonies and opinions including Simon Peter's account of God giving his Holy Spirit to the Gentiles, James posits that God's work among the Gentiles fulfills Amos's prophesy. Therefore, he recommends that the church not burden non-Jews who are turning to God. Instead, the church should only require of them what the Law requires of Gentiles living in Israel (15:15–21).

James specifically quotes a Greek translation of Amos. This text reads "Edom" as "Adam" (which in Hebrew can signify all of humanity and is often translated as "mankind") and "possess" as "seek." In Hebrew, these words closely resemble each other. These changes certainly magnify the literal sense of the original. Yet both editions maintain that only God can integrate the nations into his people. James contends that this is exactly what God is doing in and through Jesus. The rest of the church agrees. So, they send people out to join God and fulfill Jesus' commission to "make disciples of all nations" (Matt. 28:19). At some point, God sent someone to us, and now he sends us to others.

1. Who shared the gospel and discipled you? What did they do or say?

2. Who are you currently discipling? How are you teaching this person to follow Jesus?

FIVE

The Last Word

Amos 9:13–15 *"The days are coming," declares the* Lord,

"when the reaper will be overtaken by the plowman and the planter by the one treading grapes. New wine will drip from the mountains and flow from all the hills, ¹⁴and I will bring my people Israel back from exile.

"They will rebuild the ruined cities and live in them. They will plant vineyards and drink their wine; they will make gardens and eat their fruit. ¹⁵I will plant Israel in their own land, never again to be uprooted from the land I have given them," says the Lord *your God.*

Amos 5:11 *You levy a straw tax on the poor and impose a tax on their grain. Therefore, though you have built stone mansions, you will not live in them; though you have planted lush vineyards, you will not drink their wine.*

Key Observation. Sin does not speak the last word in Amos or in our lives; the Lord our God does!

Understanding the Word. This is it! Over the past eight weeks, we've examined Amos and his world (1:1; 7:12–15). We've identified his theme and considered how prophecy works (1:2–3a). We've seen how the oracles against the nations set up God's judgment of Israel's sanctuaries, courts, and rich citizens for abandoning him and oppressing the poor (1:3–2:6). We've analyzed the words (3:1–5:17) and woes (5:18–6:14) Amos declares on the Lord's behalf. We've explored Amos's visions (7:1–8:3) and pondered Israel's demise (8:4–14). Finally, we've wrestled with the inevitability of God's wrath, and we've been surprised by a future hope for God's people (9:1–11).

Amos ends with a second oracle of salvation that foresees an abundant and permanent future for Israel (9:13–15). God promises to return his people from exile and reverse his previous judgments. However, he makes a subtle but critical adjustment. The Lord does not promise that the wealthy elite will rebuild their stone mansions and replant their vineyards (5:11). Instead, he declares that *his people* will rebuild their *cities* and live in them; *they* will plant vineyards and drink their wine (Amos 9:14; Isaiah 65:21–22; Jeremiah 31:5). When God restores Israel, he will eliminate economic inequality, and everyone will prosper.

In the coming days, Israel will experience unfathomable harvests. With the threats of crop disease (4:9), locusts (4:9; 7:1), and famine (4:7; 8:11) behind them, Israel will still be gathering its grain and treading its grapes when it is time to prepare the land for the next season's crops (Leviticus 26:5). These activities would typically be separated by several months, but in the future, they will overlap. Israel will always have fields to plow, vines to plant, food to eat, and wine to drink (Joel 3:18). More importantly, the Lord will permanently replant Israel in her land (9:15). He will bring Israel home, root her in the land, and remove the threat of a future exile. Then she will be the fruitful vineyard that God always wanted (Psalm 80:8–11; Isaiah 5:1–2; 27:2–6).

In these final verses, the Lord graciously reminds Israel and us that beyond judgment, hope remains. Throughout Amos, God takes sin seriously, and sin has serious consequences. The Lord does not overlook or downplay the gravity of immoral acts or the impact of these actions on others; he definitively and completely condemns them. Yet, when our love fails, God's love remains steadfast. Our sin does not win. It does not speak the last word in Amos or in our lives; the Lord our God does!

The last word God speaks is not merely a word of salvation, it is a word of culmination. Not only will God return and restore Israel, but he will fulfill his promises and complete his plans. He will not simply recover what was, but he will establish something better—something new. This is the great hope of the Christian faith. We look forward to the day when God will make everything new again—when he will remake his creation, resurrect our bodies, destroy death, and dwell with us forever (Revelation 21:1–5).

1. What aspect(s) of God's great renewal stand out to you? Why?

2. What specific things has God revealed to you through Amos? How will you think and live differently in light of this study?

WEEK EIGHT

GATHERING DISCUSSION OUTLINE

A. Open session in prayer.

B. View this week's video.

C. What general impressions and thoughts do you have after watching the video and reading the daily writings on these Scriptures? What, specifically, did this week's passages teach you about faith, life, and prayer?

D. Discuss selected questions from the daily readings. Always invite class members to share key insights or to raise questions that they found to be the most meaningful.

1. **KEY OBSERVATION**: God's presence is limitless; it extends even to the places we least expect.

   DISCUSSION QUESTION: Where in your life do you not expect God's presence? Why?

2. **KEY OBSERVATION:** God displays his incomparable power through the perceived weakness of sacrificial love.

   DISCUSSION QUESTION: In what tangible ways can you display the self-giving love of God to others this week?

3. **KEY OBSERVATION:** God always and only saves us by his grace.

   DISCUSSION QUESTION: What pebbles and branches does the Lord want to sift out of your life?

4. **KEY OBSERVATION:** In and through Jesus, God does what Amos prophesies—he incorporates the nations into his family.

   DISCUSSION QUESTION: Who are you currently discipling? How are you teaching this person to follow Jesus?

5. **KEY OBSERVATION:** Sin does not speak the last word in Amos or in our lives; the Lord our God does!

   DISCUSSION QUESTION: What specific things has God revealed to you through Amos? How will you think and live differently in light of this study?

E. Close session with prayer.